HURRAH FOR
LIBERALS

How Progressives Defeated Conservatives to Create Democracy, Human Rights and Safe Modern Life

James A. Haught

ISBN 978-1530252176

CreateSpace

Cover by Adam Howell

Thomas Jefferson, Abraham Lincoln, Frederick Douglass, Margaret Sanger, Theodore Roosevelt, Franklin Roosevelt, Martin Luther King Jr. and Lyndon Johnson

Images from Wikimedia Commons and Library of Congress.

Contents

For Nancy, Joel, Jake, Jeb, Cass, Phil, John, Karolyn, Gwenna, Helen, Ben, Lori, Sam, Lyndsey, Lisa, Michele, Brad, Zach, Brittani, Jonathan, Ian, Conner, Katie and all my clan

Tide of history flows left

In the three centuries since The Enlightenment, western civilization has made enormous social progress. Democracy, human rights, personal liberties and family well-being have blossomed. Life gradually became more decent and humane.

Nearly all this cultural improvement was achieved by reform-minded liberals who defeated conservatives defending former hierarchies, privileges and inequalities. Look at the historical record of painful social struggles that ended with progressive victories:

Conservatives tried to retain slavery, but they lost.

They tried to block voting by women, but lost.

They tried to prevent couples from using birth control, but lost.

They tried to obstruct Social Security pensions for oldsters and the disabled, but lost.

They tried to outlaw labor unions, but lost.

They tried to prevent unemployment compensation for the jobless, but lost.

They tried to block workers compensation for on-the-job injuries, but lost.

They tried to keep stores closed on the Sabbath, but lost.

They tried to sustain Prohibition of alcohol, but lost.

They opposed policing of stock market abuses, but lost.

They opposed food stamps for the poor, but lost.

They defended racial segregation, but lost.

They supported government-led prayer in school, but lost.

They tried to continue throwing gays in prison, but lost.

They tried to defeat Medicare and Medicaid, but lost.

They tried to halt the sexual revolution, but lost.

They fought against equal human rights laws, but lost.

They tried to censor sexy magazines, books and movies, but lost.

They sought to jail girls and doctors who end pregnancies, but lost.

They tried to block liquor clubs and lotteries, but lost.

They tried to prevent expansion of health insurance through the Affordable Care Act, but lost.

They tried to halt same-sex marriage, but lost.

Progress of civilization depends largely on successful crusades by political and social liberals who struggle -- sometimes for centuries -- before triumphing over conservative resistance.

One of my history-minded friends has a long-range political view summed up in three words: Liberals always win. Battles may be ferocious and seem endless, he says, but they finally bring progressive victories. Once a human-rights breakthrough is accomplished, it locks into the roster of democratic freedoms, almost never to be revoked.

The struggle to end slavery was an epic battle. Generations of abolitionist clamor and the horrible Civil War were required, but they finally moved America to a higher level of decency.

Similarly, suffragettes strove almost a century before they enabled American women to vote.

And it took a half-century for American couples to win the right to practice birth control. Planned Parenthood founder Margaret Sanger was jailed eight times for the crime of mentioning sex -- but she eventually transformed society. A Supreme Court victory in 1965 struck down contraceptive bans for married couples, and a follow-up victory in 1972 erased them for unwed couples. Liberals won, conservatives lost.

The nonviolent civil rights movement that wiped out Jim Crow segregation and made Dr. Martin Luther King Jr. an American icon was a classic liberal victory.

Of course, history doesn't move in a clear, predictable manner. Germany was advanced and modern, yet it sank into the horrors of Nazism. Other setbacks occur. But the overall tide of civilization flows in a progressive direction.

In his landmark book, *The Better Angels of Our Nature: Why Violence has Declined,* Harvard psychologist Steven Pinker concludes that all sorts of human evils -- war, genocide, murder, rape, torture, dueling, wife-bashing, attacks on minorities, etc. -- have faded enormously from the Western world. International warfare has virtually vanished in the 21st century. Pursuit of such humane goals lies at the heart of the liberal agenda.

When I first became a news reporter in the 1950s, conservative Bible Belt morality was enforced by laws. It was a crime for stores to open on the Sabbath. It was a crime to look at the equivalent of a *Playboy* magazine, or to read a sexy book. (Our mayor once sent police to raid bookstores selling *Peyton Place.*)

Back then, it was a felony to be gay, and those who were caught were sent to prison under old sodomy laws. Back then, it was a felony for a desperate girl to end a pregnancy. It was illegal for an unmarried couple to share a bedroom. Divorce or unwed pregnancy was an unmentionable disgrace. Jews weren't allowed into Christian-only country clubs. Public schools had mandatory teacher-led prayer. It was a crime to buy a cocktail or a lottery ticket.

African Americans were confined to poor ghettos, forbidden to enter white schools, white restaurants, white hotels, white theaters, white swimming pools, white neighborhoods -- or white employment. Society had a cruel apartheid system.

That world disappeared, decade after decade. The culture slowly evolved. Sunday "blue laws" were undone. Teacher-led prayers were banned. Gay sex became legal. Liquor clubs were approved. Abortion became legal. State governments became lottery operators. Censorship ended. The historic civil rights movement wiped out segregation. Other conservative taboos and barriers gradually disappeared.

Within my lifetime, morality and customs flip-flopped. Conservative thou-shalt-nots lost their grip on society. Liberals won -- yet it happened so gradually that few noticed.

For several decades, the strongest indicator of politics was church membership. White evangelicals voted overwhelmingly for Mitt Romney. People who don't attend worship voted overwhelmingly for Barack Obama. The latter became the largest group in the Democratic Party base. They're more tolerant.

Today, survey after survey finds American church membership fading, while the young generation ignores religion. Sociologists think the secular trend is unstoppable. People who say their faith is "none" already comprise one-fourth of the adult population -- 56 million Americans -- and they seem destined someday to be the largest segment. The social tide is flowing away from conservative fundamentalism and its Puritanical agenda, toward liberal tolerance. Racial acceptance likewise is growing, mostly erasing the two-tier society I knew as a youth.

All these factors support the liberals-always-win maxim. The progressive worldview is called humanism -- trying to make life better for all people -- and it's a powerful current. In 1960, John F. Kennedy said in a famed speech:

"If by a 'liberal' they mean someone who looks ahead and not behind, someone who welcomes new ideas without rigid reaction, someone who cares about the welfare of the people -- their health, their housing, their schools, their jobs, their civil rights and their civil liberties ...then I'm proud to say that I'm a liberal."

Now that progressives have won the battle for same-sex marriage and locked the Affordable Care Act into law, the never-ending struggle undoubtedly will shift to new fronts. Maybe legalization of marijuana or registration of pistols or free college will be the next big showdown. Whatever comes, I'm ready to predict the eventual winner.

Nobel Peace Prize-winner Martin Luther King Jr. said: "The arc of the moral universe is long, but it bends toward justice." However, some University of Michigan scholars concluded that the notion of "the right side of history" is a myth -- there's no guarantee that future events will extend previous democratic breakthroughs. Terrible reversals could occur.

Nonetheless, the transformation that began with The Enlightenment is a fact. Amid all the chaos and confusion of daily life, through a thousand contradictory barrages, the struggle for a safer, fairer, more secure, more humane world never ceases.

Clear differences

In tumultuous sociopolitical struggles, a frequent pattern is visible: Conservatives often fight to preserve their own wealth or privileges, but liberals battle for causes that don't enrich or benefit themselves personally.

This fact is clear in the long crusade to abolish slavery, and in never-ending attempts to aid the poor. Liberals are less driven by self-interest, more driven to help the entire society. Conservatives are impelled more by a desire to help themselves.

Famed economist John Kenneth Galbraith wrote: "The modern conservative is engaged in one of man's oldest exercises in moral philosophy: that is, the search for a superior moral justification for selfishness."

Consider other obvious differences between conservatives and liberals:

First, economics: Inherited wealth is a factor in right-wing politics. While most people hope to accumulate affluence and leave it for their children, this goal is especially strong among conservatives. They lobby to eliminate the estate tax on big holdings.

Conservatives feel less empathy for left-out families, those not born into privilege, those less-endowed with abilities for success. Conservatives constantly seek to pay less in taxes that fund the government safety net for unlucky folks. A frequent right-wing accusation is that progressives want to "redistribute wealth."

Second, morality: Conservatives generally adhere to supernatural religion and its sexual taboos. They usually support censorship to ban sex from movies, television, books, magazines, and the like. Vestiges of narrow-minded colonial Puritanism linger.

An Australian, whose nation originated as a penal colony, reportedly told an American: "We're the lucky ones. We got the criminals, and you got the Puritans."

Actress Elizabeth Taylor was quoted: "The problem with people who have no vices is that generally you can be sure they're going to have some pretty annoying virtues."

Conservative morality includes a belief that highly religious employers should be allowed to deny birth control to their female employees -- and that such corporate owners will lose their "religious freedom" if health insurance plans of their firms cover contraception.

Conservative morality includes a belief that every human egg acquires a soul the moment it is fertilized, therefore it is murder to destroy a microscopic zygote. As a result, many conservatives oppose medical research that extracts stem cells from frozen fertilized eggs.

Third, militarism: Conservatives tend to be "hawks" suspicious of unfamiliar people, and quicker to use armed force to kill presumed enemies. In contrast, television commentator Chris Matthews voiced a liberal view when he said: "I think that the horror of war is so vital to realize, to take into our own minds and hearts, that we don't send men and women into battle until the leaders fully and fairly decide that is the only solution."

Nobel Prize-winning martyr Martin Luther King Jr. wrote: "A nation that continues year after year to spend more money on military defense than on programs of social uplift is approaching spiritual doom."

Even moderate Republican President Dwight Eisenhower famously said: "Every gun that is made, every warship launched, every rocket fired, signifies in the final sense a theft from those who hunger and are not fed, those who are cold and are not clothed."

Fourth, equality: Conservatives don't seem to care if inferior status is imposed on people with darker skin or foreign accents, or on women, or on gays, or other minorities. Right-wingers traditionally endorse hierarchies that favor privileged whites like themselves, and cast everyone else into the cellar. Racial segregation and gated sanctuaries are a manifestation of conservatism.

Fifth, justice: Conservatives usually support the death penalty and other harsh punishments. The fact that execution is inflicted chiefly on black and poor defendants doesn't seem to trouble them.

Singer Paul Simon said: "The death penalty is reserved for people who do not have enough money to defend themselves."

Laws and police enforcement frequently seem designed to prevent the rabble from bothering the elite. The witty French cynic Anatole France (1844-1924) lampooned: "The law, in its majestic equality, forbids rich and poor alike to sleep under bridges, beg in the streets, or steal bread."

Sixth, pollution: Conservatives tend to ignore industrial pollution, while liberals clamor for cleanups. This conflict is especially intense in debates over global warming, caused by carbon fumes that form a "greenhouse" layer in the sky, trapping heat on Earth's surface. Many right-wing folks claim that the warm-up is a myth.

Seventh, guns: The right to bear arms is a crucial plank in the Republican platform. America's horrendous gun murder rate and recurring massacres spur liberals to seek safety laws such as universal background checks for all pistol-buyers. But conservatives and the powerful gun lobby often block such precautions.

Eighth, abortion: Terminating pregnancies remains a "hot-button" issue. The 1973 *Roe v. Wade* Supreme Court ruling that let American women and girls choose abortion still infuriates many "pro-life" conservatives, who consider it homicide to halt pregnancy. Even pro-life murder occurs when religious extremists kill doctors or nurses at abortion clinics.

Ninth, gays: Ostracizing homosexuals is a long-running conservative theme, dating back to the Bible, which commands: "If a man also lie with mankind, as he lieth with a woman, both of them have committed an abomination: they shall surely be put to death; their blood shall be upon them."

Gays have no control over their orientation, and are blameless for it, yet they have been persecuted, imprisoned, even killed, for centuries because many "straights" are repulsed by them. Finally, in the 21st century, western liberals at last are securing safety and public acceptance of them.

"All America loses when any person is denied or forced out of a job because of sexual orientation," President Bill Clinton said.

Left-right splits crop up in many other forms: (1) Liberals are more inclined to give citizenship to Hispanic aliens who sneaked into the country to find work; hard-line conservatives want to catch and deport them all. (2) Liberals lean toward international government through the United Nations; but conservatives defend America's "sovereignty." (3) Many conservatives think America is "exceptional" and favored by God; but liberals mostly see the United States as a nation like other democracies. (4) Most liberals want separation of church and state, to prevent coercive abuses by the majority faith; but conservatives try to blur the line, for example, by giving tax-paid vouchers so religious parents can send their children to church schools at taxpayer cost. (5) Liberals generally support affirmative action that helps minorities overcome past discrimination; but conservatives claim this gives unfair advantage to blacks. (6) Many progressives support physician-assisted suicide for terminal patients who want to escape pain and hopelessness; but conservatives generally oppose it. (7)

Liberals want to decriminalize marijuana usage and ease the "war on drugs"; but conservatives generally back hard penalties. (8) Left-leaning Americans generally think health treatment should be a human right for everyone; but conservatives in Congress voted sixty times to kill the Affordable Care Act, and many Republican governors and state legislators refuse to expand Medicaid for lower-income families. (9) Liberals want to make college free or low-cost; but conservatives oppose higher taxes to fund such a plan.

In recent decades, various psychologists and brain researchers have analyzed innate differences between liberals and conservatives. Brain functions of the two groups have been found to vary significantly. Apparently, the gulf between left and right is wired into human genetics.

University of Virginia psychologist Jonathan Haidt wrote a 2012 book titled *The Righteous Mind: Why Good People are Divided by Politics and Religion.* He cites research implying that progressives focus strongly on three issues: social fairness, personal liberty, and caring for the weak. Conservatives partly share those urges, he says, but they also focus on three others: sanctity, respect for authority, and loyalty -- qualities that breed political and religious conformity.

Dr. Haidt says conservatives react more strongly to perceived threats, and are more revolted by disgusting images. He says liberalism can be traced back to kindergarten age, when tots destined to be left-wingers display more curiosity and verbal abilities, but are less neat and obedient.

Stand-up comedian Mort Sahl said: "Liberals feel unworthy of their possessions. Conservatives feel they deserve everything they've stolen."

Obviously, ingrained differences drive America's never-ending political and cultural battles. Bottom line: Conservatives want to make life better for themselves and their children. Liberals of course want the same, but they also strive to improve life for everyone.

Liberal role model

Jesus was a liberal. He sided with underdogs. He championed little people, not the privileged and powerful. "Blessed are the poor" was one of his maxims. He told a noble: "Sell all that thou hast, and distribute unto the poor." His teachings were virtually a prescription for the compassionate public safety net upholding people and families in modern democracies:

"For I was hungered, and ye gave me meat. I was thirsty, and ye gave me drink. I was a stranger, and ye took me in. Naked, and ye clothed me. I was sick, and ye visited me. I was in prison, and ye came unto me.... Inasmuch as ye have done it unto one of the least of these my brethren, ye have done it unto me."

He also said: "When thou makest a feast, call the poor, the maimed, the lame, the blind: and thou shalt be blessed, for they cannot recompense thee."

His parable of the Good Samaritan spotlighted the nobility of caring for victims of misfortune. His Golden Rule -- "All things whatsoever ye would that men should do to you, do ye even so to them" -- underscored common fairness.

Jesus didn't support harsh punishments. When the law demanded stoning of an adulteress, he famously said: "He that is without sin among you, let him first cast a stone at her."

Jesus advocated separation of church and state. "Render therefore unto Caesar the things which be Caesar's, and unto God the things which be God's."

Jesus wasn't a militarist. "Blessed are the peacemakers" was another of his maxims.

Thomas Jefferson was so impressed by these humanitarian guidelines that he clipped and pasted them into a renowned "Jefferson Bible," discarding supernatural claims of the New Testament. In a letter to John Adams, Jefferson called Christ's compassionate teachings "the most sublime and benevolent code of morals which has ever been offered to man."

Clearly, without question, Jesus espoused values aligned with the modern political left. Sometimes, this facet of religion is called the "social gospel."

So it's strange that America's white evangelicals and fundamentalists are the bedrock of the Republican Party -- a party that favors the rich, undercuts the safety net, backs militarism, and demands harsher justice and the death penalty. Oddly, these conservative believers contradict the values of Jesus.

When George W. Bush was governor of Texas, he signed execution warrants for a record-breaking 135 inmates, including 11 who were juveniles at the time of the crimes. Many cases involved questionable evidence. Yet Bush was renowned as a born-again believer and declared on national television that his favorite philosopher was Jesus. The contrast between the two triggers clanging bells of cognitive dissonance.

Meanwhile, secular Americans who don't attend church have become a bulwark of the Democratic Party, which supports the safety net for average folks. How odd that churchless people are closer to the social principles of Jesus than many churchgoers are.

The new Pope Francis gained worldwide popularity because he pushes the humane ideals of Jesus, not the sexual taboos and hidebound Puritanism that dominated his church in the past.

"Inequality is the root of social evil," Francis declares. All poor families deserve "land, lodging, labor," he preaches. He says capitalism rests on "unfettered pursuit of money" and discards "unproductive people" like the poor, elderly and less-educated.

Conservatives are rattled by the pontiff. Republican figure Pat Buchanan accused him of preaching "socialist sermons."

But the pope is merely voicing the values of Jesus. He is underscoring what should be obvious to every thinking person: that Jesus was a liberal.

Russian leader Mikhail Gorbachev said: "Jesus was the first socialist, the first to seek a better life for mankind."

Jesus touched a vein of empathy deep inside most people, and framed the cause of liberal compassion.

Modern liberalism born

Values that later grew into liberalism began stirring in the epoch now known as The Enlightenment, starting more than three centuries ago, chiefly in England and France. It was an era when kings still ruled brutally by "divine right," and the church still sought to execute "heretics" holding irregular beliefs, or jail skeptics for blasphemy. Most people were agricultural serfs, working on lands inherited by wealthy barons and counts. The bottom-rung majority had virtually no rights.

But The Enlightenment roused a new way of thinking: a sense that all people should have some control over their lives, a voice in their own destiny. Absolute power of authorities -- either the throne or the cathedral -- was challenged. Reformers asserted that human reason and the scientific method can improve society and benefit nearly everyone.

The 1600s were a time of ugly intolerance, much of it stemming from alliances between church and throne. In England's notorious Star Chamber, controlled by the Anglican archbishop, Puritan and Presbyterian dissenters were forced to testify against themselves, then sentenced to have their ears cut off or their faces branded with markings such as S.L. (for seditious libeler). One victim, John Lilburne, became a public hero because he wrote pamphlets claiming that all people deserved "freeborn rights" not subject to king or church.

Europe was emerging from horrors of religious wars and massacres between Catholics and Protestants. Catholic France persecuted Huguenot Protestants. Jews were attacked cruelly and banned from certain nations, including England. Sporadic executions of "heretics" and "witches" still occurred. England's last accused witch was put to death in 1684. A few others were executed around Europe and the New World for another century.

This was the background that helped spawn Enlightenment reform.

England was shattered by civil war in the 1640s between Parliament and Puritans on one side versus King Charles I and Anglicans on the other. Charles was beheaded and the power of kings was reduced -- expanding an erosion that began four centuries earlier when barons forced King John to sign the Magna Carta yielding certain rights.

By the late 1600s, some thinkers began pondering society and government:

Thomas Hobbes (1588-1679) wrote *Leviathan* asserting that people need a "social contract" to secure safe lives. In a dog-eat-dog natural state, he said, everyone suffers from "continual fear and danger of violent death; and the life of man [is] solitary, poor, nasty, brutish and short." Therefore, he said, people must yield power to a sovereign government to enforce order and protect them. Hobbes supported a king as the sovereign -- but the tide away from absolute kings already was flowing. Hobbes raised awareness that the social order is made by humans, not by God.

In his many writings, Hobbes repeatedly affronted the clergy. A bishop accused him of atheism, possibly punishable by death. The allegation subsided, then flared again. Nearing eighty, Hobbes hastily burned some of his papers and eluded prosecution.

John Locke (1632-1704) hatched notions of democracy, arguing that all people, male and female, deserve a degree of equality. He dismissed the divine right of kings, and advocated separation of church and state to avert religious conflict.

John Milton (1608-1674) was more than an epic poet who wrote in four languages. He also supported popular government and attacked state-mandated religion. When Parliament imposed censorship on writings, he defied a licensing requirement and published an *Areopagitica* pamphlet claiming that all thinking people are entitled to free expression of their beliefs. "Books are not absolutely dead things," he said. "He who destroys a good book kills reason itself." The principle of free speech and free press was furthered.

In France, Baron de Montesquieu (1689-1755) championed democracy and envisioned an elected government with power divided between executive, legislative and judicial branches.

Francois Marie Arouet (1694-1788) -- "that consuming fire called Voltaire," as Will Durant called him -- was a brilliant French writer who became a heroic champion of human rights. Endlessly, he denounced cruelties of bishops and aristocrats. Here's an example:

In the devout town of Abbeville, a teen-age youth, Francois de la Barre, was accused of marring a crucifix, singing impious songs and wearing his hat while a church procession passed. He was sentenced to have his tongue torn out, his head chopped off, and his remains burned. Voltaire wrote bitter protests against this savagery. He helped appeal the youth's case to Parliament, which showed "mercy" by affording the blasphemer a quick death by beheading -- with a copy of Voltaire's *Philosophical Dictionary* nailed to his body.

Voltaire's protest writings roused ferment across Europe and won reversal of a few cases. He freed Jean Espinas, who had spent twenty-three years aboard a penal galley ship because he sheltered a fugitive Protestant minister for one night. Likewise, he freed Claude Chaumont from a galley bench, where he had been sentenced for attending a Protestant worship service.

In *The Rights of Man*, Thomas Paine wrote that Voltaire's "forte lay in exposing and ridiculing the superstitions which priestcraft, united with statecraft, had interwoven with governments."

At first, Enlightenment ideas were somewhat suppressed in Europe, where kings and archbishops still prevailed, but they found fertile ground in America's colonies. Brilliant radicals such as Thomas Jefferson, John Adams, Benjamin Franklin and James Madison read them ardently and adopted them as a pattern for the first modern democracy, the

United States of America. In the Declaration of Independence, Jefferson summed up the essence:

"All men are created equal and endowed by their creator with certain inalienable rights, among these life, liberty and the pursuit of happiness."

Less-known founding father George Mason incorporated the principles into the Bill of Rights, keeping church and state apart, guaranteeing free speech, and protecting each person from abuses by the majority. Similarly, the personal liberties were reiterated in the Rights of Man and the Citizen adopted by the French Revolution, and eventually in the Universal Declaration of Human Rights that Eleanor Roosevelt helped craft for the United Nations.

The Enlightenment was the seedbed that sprouted most of the liberal freedoms now enjoyed in democracies everywhere. It projected a model for humane, safe, fair modern life.

Free speech and press

Free speech and free press mean the same thing: the right to voice any beliefs or ideas, even unpopular ones -- orally or on paper -- without fear of being punished for it. Sometimes it's called freedom of expression. Through history, various advances slowly won this right, which lies at the very heart of democracy. It's all about the right to think freely, safe from arrest or prosecution.

Some ancient Greeks and Romans first proposed tolerance of differing viewpoints. In 1501, Pope Alexander XI of the notorious Borgias ordered censorship of unwanted ideas. The church's famed *Index Expurgatorius,* listing banned books, was launched in 1559 and continued for centuries, eventually forbidding believers to read works of Rene Descartes, Galileo, David Hume, John Locke, Daniel Defoe, Jean-Jacques Rousseau, Voltaire and many other thinkers. In France, printer-scholar Etienne Dolet was burned at the stake in 1546 for his unorthodox writings. England's infamous Star Chamber, which tortured and mutilated nonconformists, also censored printed material.

In 1644, poet John Milton's *Aeropagitica* appeal to Parliament opposed censorship of writings. "Give me the liberty to know, to utter, and to argue freely according to conscience, above all liberties," he wrote.

Years ago, a former dean of West Virginia State University, Edwin Hoffman, wrote a superb book titled *Pathways to Freedom*, outlining several breakthroughs of democracy. He gave this example:

In the 1730s, after England seized New Amsterdam from the Dutch and renamed it New York, a new British governor was sent to the colony. He turned out to be a greedy, arrogant tyrant seeking to enrich himself. Many New Yorkers turned against him. A few started a little newspaper, *The New York Weekly Journal*, to express their concerns. It was printed by a German immigrant, John Peter Zenger.

The paper didn't dare criticize the governor openly, but it published vague warnings without using his name. Nonetheless, the governor ordered Zenger arrested on charges of inflaming the people against the crown. The printer was locked in a cell for nine months, but continued publishing his weekly by dictating to his wife and friends through a hole in the door.

When his case finally came to trial, an aging Quaker lawyer from Philadelphia eloquently argued that people should have a right to criticize authorities. To the surprise of nearly everyone, including the defense, jurors quickly declared Zenger innocent, even though he had admitted printing the criticisms. New York townspeople hailed him as a hero.

It was a small landmark in the struggle for freedom of speech and press, which later were locked into the First Amendment of America's Bill of Rights and subsequent democracy codes.

Free speech and press are bedrock principles for liberals, and have been for centuries. Crusading newspaper columnist Heywood Broun (1888-1939) once said: "Free speech is about as good a cause as the world has ever known."

Supreme Court Justice Oliver Wendell Holmes Jr. (1841-1935) said: "The very aim of our institutions is just this: that we may think what we like and say what we think."

Yale University President and historian Alfred Whitney Griswold (1906-1963) wrote in *Essays on Education*: "Books won't stay banned…. Ideas won't go to jail. In the long run of history, the censor and the inquisitor have always lost."

Singer Harry Belafonte said: "You can cage the singer but not the song."

Philosopher-lecturer Ralph Waldo Emerson (1803-1882) wrote: "Whenever they burn books they will also, in the end, burn people."

The American Library Association and Association of American Publishers said jointly:

"The freedom to read is essential to our democracy. It is continuously under attack. Private groups and public authorities in various parts of the country are working to remove books from sale, to censor textbooks, to label 'controversial' books, to distribute lists of 'objectionable' books or authors, and to purge libraries."

America's First Amendment forbids any law "abridging the freedom of speech, or of the press" -- yet conservatives spent centuries trying to banish sex from written or spoken acknowledgement.

Historically, prudish censors banned writings by Charles Baudelaire, Gustave Flaubert, Honore de Balzac, James Joyce, D.H. Lawrence, Henry Miller, Samuel Beckett, the Marquis de Sade and numerous others. An 1897 court ruling declared a newspaper called the *Chicago Dispatch* "obscene, lewd, lascivious and indecent." The 1760 novel *Fanny Hill* by John Cleland was outlawed in Boston as late as 1966.

Sex censorship peaked in the late 1800s under priggish Anthony Comstock (1844-1915), a Civil War veteran who had been offended by coarse language of fellow Union soldiers. In 1873 Comstock created the New York Society for the Suppression of Vice and began a lifelong career of stamping out sex.

That same year, he induced Congress to pass the notorious Comstock Law banning "obscene, lewd or lascivious" material from the mail or other public venues. It also outlawed mentions of birth control, abortion, venereal disease and the like. It even prevented anatomy textbooks from being mailed to medical students.

Comstock was made a postal inspector with a right to carry a pistol. He became a dynamo attacking and harassing all writers who mentioned sex. He called himself "a weeder in God's garden."

When Ida Craddock wrote marriage manuals containing sexual details, Comstock had her sentenced to federal prison. She committed suicide on the eve of reporting to jail.

Comstock alerted police about a George Bernard Shaw play, *Mrs. Warren's Profession*, and called Shaw an "Irish smut dealer." Shaw replied that "Comstockery is the world's standing joke at the expense of the United States." He said it makes Europeans see America as "a provincial place, a second-rate, country-town civilization after all."

Comstock repeatedly prosecuted Margaret Sanger, founder of Planned Parenthood, for advocating birth control. He boasted that he caused 4,000 arrests, drove fifteen people to suicide, destroyed fifteen tons of books and 284,000 pounds of plates for printing books.

Conservative sexual censorship continued for decades in America. In 1940, publisher Jacob Brussel reprinted Henry Miller's *Tropic of Cancer* describing his sex life as an American in France in the 1930s. Brussel was thrown into prison for three years. In 1961, Grove Press again printed the book and was forced to spend $100,000 fighting sixty censorship cases. Pennsylvania's supreme court ruled that it is "not a book. It is a cesspool, an open sewer, a pit of putrefaction, a slimy gathering of all that is rotten in the debris of human depravity." However, in 1964, the Supreme Court ruled in *Grove Press Inc. v. Gerstein* that *Cancer* isn't obscene.

In subsequent rulings, the high court declared that sexual materials can be banned only if they violate three standards: (1) they appeal to prurient interest in ways that breach "contemporary community standards," (2) they are presented in "a patently offensive way" and (3) the entire work "lacks serious literary, artistic, political or scientific value." Since then, obscenity prosecutions have declined in America, and the Internet brought a flood of explicit sex of every imaginable sort.

Finally, a horrible new type of censorship -- killing writers and publishers -- emerged in the current era of faith-based slaughter.

Islam is based on a belief that the angel Gabriel dictated the Quran to Muhammad -- but in 1988 Muslim-born novelist Salman Rushdie wrote *The Satanic Verses*, which contains dream scenes subtly lampooning the faith's basic claim. Muslims around the world exploded in rage and rioting. The Ayatollah Khomeini of Iran issued a *fatwa* calling on Muslims to murder Rushdie and his publishers. Iran posted million-dollar rewards for any killers. The author was hidden with round-the-clock police protection, but one of his translators was stabbed to death and two others wounded. In 1993 at Sivas, Turkey, a mob of worshippers from a mosque attacked a hotel hosting an arts conference that featured a writer who had attempted to publish Rushdie's book. Enraged attackers set fire to the hotel and killed thirty-seven people.

Another example: A satirical French magazine, *Charlie Hebdo*, repeatedly mocked

Islam in writings and cartoons. In early 2015 armed Muslim attackers stormed the publication's Paris office and killed a dozen people. Various other religion-driven murders -- a supreme form of censorship -- have occurred.

Free speech and press are a central liberal ideal, but they can incur danger under this new menace.

Freedom of religion

Religion has a terrible side-effect: It causes some believers to kill people holding different beliefs. Western history teems with ugly examples.

Two centuries of Christian Crusades were waged against Muslim "infidels" in the Mideast, killing multitudes but accomplishing little. Muslims retained control.

As Crusader armies assembled for marches to the Mideast, they first decided to kill "the infidels among us," European Jews. Many massacres occurred in ghettos filled with despised people the Crusaders called "Christ-killers."

Afterward, European Jews were persecuted, banished, executed and slaughtered by Christians sporadically for a millennium. The Inquisition tortured and burned Jewish converts suspected of backsliding to their old faith. Rumors spread that Jews were kidnapping Christian babies and sacrificing them -- and this "blood libel" triggered many massacres. Similarly, rumors said Jews were stealing host wafers from churches and driving nails through them to crucify Jesus again -- and this absurd falsehood caused more killings. During the Black Death plague, superstitious Christians said Jews were poisoning wells, which brought more slaughter. Intermittent Jew-killing continued through Russia's pogroms in the early 1900s -- and set the public mood for the Nazi Holocaust of World War II.

The Holy Inquisition tortured and burned thousands of "heretics" for holding nonconformist beliefs. Likewise, Inquisition witch-hunters tortured and burned uncountable women suspected of copulating with Satan, flying through the sky, changing into animals, blighting crops, and the like.

Bloody Hussite wars -- forerunners to the Reformation -- were fought partly over the Catholic Church's claim that the miracle of transubstantiation changes communion wine and wafers into Christ's actual blood and flesh.

The Reformation loosed much-worse wars between Catholics and Protestants. French Catholics and Huguenots slaughtered each other in a recurring series called the Wars of Religion (which included the notorious St. Bartholomew's Day massacre of Huguenots). England's Catholic "Bloody Mary" executed throngs of Protestants. Switzerland suffered Canton Wars between the two faiths. A final convulsion was the Thirty Years War that killed half the population of Germany.

Persecution of small sects like Anabaptists was ferocious. Hundreds were killed because they favored adult baptism over infant baptism.

Many thinkers were put to death. Physician-scholar Michael Servetus, who discovered the pulmonary circulation of blood, was burned at the stake in Calvinist Geneva in 1553 for doubting the Trinity. His own books were used for his pyre. (Teens at my Unitarian church hold a "Michael Servetus weenie roast" yearly in his honor.) Philosopher-scientist Giordano Bruno was burned at the stake in Rome in 1600 for teaching that the universe is infinite, with many stars that might be accompanied by planets, even some with alien life.

After centuries of killing each other over religion, modern Europeans strangely decided that religion is unimportant. Today, churchgoing has almost vanished among educated Western Europeans.

However, religious killing still occurs through today's Islamic "cult of death." Endlessly, Sunni and Shiite suicide volunteers become human bombs or perform "martyrdom missions" to kill rival believers or Western "infidels." They sacrifice their own lives to murder others in the name of God. Massacres by al-Qaida, the Islamic State, Boko Haram, al-Shabaab, Hezbollah, Hamas, Islamic Jihad, Fatah al-Islam and other armed fanatic groups fill the news almost daily. Shiites in Iran still murder and persecute adherents of the small Baha'i sect, which arose in the 1800s from a mystic who declared that he was the long-awaited messiah of all faiths, returning at last.

In the long chronicle of faith-based slaughter, here's an example that helped establish freedom of religion:

When Quakers first began expressing their personal, emotional beliefs in the 1600s, England's ruling Puritans under Oliver Cromwell denounced and persecuted them. Many fled to the New World -- unfortunately to

35

Puritan Massachusetts, where they were persecuted anew. Massachusetts law required that all residents attend Puritan worship. In 1658 the Massachusetts legislature decreed that Quakers must be banned, on pain of death. Quakers arriving by ship were seized and jailed, and their books burned.

But Quakers stubbornly defied expulsion, returning repeatedly to hold worship services in homes. Persecution intensified. New laws decreed that Quakers would be flogged, or have their ears cut off, or their foreheads branded, or their tongues burned through by a hot iron. Any resident who sheltered a Quaker was fined -- and in one case, children of an old couple were ordered sold into slavery because the parents couldn't pay a fine for sheltering. (The punishment failed because no ship captain would transport the unlucky children.)

Quaker resistance finally forced a showdown. In 1659, three unrepentant Quakers -- Marmaduke Stevenson, William Robinson and Mary Dyer -- were tried on capital charges and sentenced to death. The two men were hanged in Boston Commons on Oct. 27, 1659, but the woman was reprieved and banished. However, she stubbornly returned to defy the Puritan law, and was hanged in 1660. The following year a fourth Quaker, William Leddra, also was hanged.

By this time, some Massachusetts Puritans were becoming revolted by the cruelty of their colony and tried to soften Quaker punishments. In 1661 King Charles II ordered the colony to halt executions. He sent a royal governor who passed a Toleration Act allowing some believers to hold unorthodox beliefs. It was a breakthrough for freedom of religion.

Peaceful acceptance of all sorts of religious views is a central belief of liberals, who contend that government shouldn't inflict prosecutions and punishments to enforce any doctrine. Separation of church and state was espoused by Enlightenment thinkers, and adopted when America's radical founders created the first modern democracy. It became locked into the First Amendment of the Bill of Rights.

Virginia's historic Statute for Religious Freedom, written by Thomas Jefferson in 1777 and finally passed in 1786, declares "that no man shall be compelled to frequent or support any religious worship, place, or ministry whatsoever, nor shall be enforced, restrained, molested, or burthened in his body or goods, nor shall otherwise suffer on account of his religious opinions or belief; but that all men shall be free to profess, and by argument to maintain, their opinion in matters of religion, and that the same shall in no wise diminish, enlarge, or affect their civil capacities."

Similar guarantees of church-state separation were written into France's Rights of Man and the Citizen, and into the Universal Declaration of Human Rights adopted by the United Nations.

By coincidence, the first Boston Quakers were hanged on October 27 -- the same calendar date that skeptic Michael Servetus was burned in Geneva. So that date eventually was adopted for International Religious

Freedom Day, one of many observations little-known to the public. Meanwhile, America has a different Religious Freedom Day, January 16, marking the date that Jefferson's statute was signed into law.

Footnote: My state of West Virginia was involved in another religious freedom breakthrough, as follows:

During the patriotic fervor of World War II, some Jehovah's Witnesses in our Mountain State enraged neighbors because they refused to salute the flag, and wouldn't let their children do so in public schools. They said their religion required them to swear allegiance only to God. Public anger caused some West Virginians to brutalize or humiliate Witness families.

Some Witness children in my town of Charleston were expelled from school for their "unpatriotic" behavior. But the American Civil Liberties Union and a fiery old Charleston lawyer named Horace Meldahl fought their case all the way to the nation's Supreme Court, which ruled in favor of the children in a famed 1943 decision (*West Virginia State Board of Education v. Barnette*). The court said personal beliefs are "beyond the reach of majorities and officials." Justice Robert H. Jackson wrote eloquently:

"If there is any fixed star in our constitutional constellation, it is that no official, high or petty, can prescribe what shall be orthodox in politics, nationalism, religion, or other matters of opinion, or force citizens to confess by word or act."

Freedom of religion is another human right that liberals secured for everyone. President Obama declared in Cairo in 2009: "Freedom of religion is central to the ability of peoples to live together."

Abolition of slavery

Today it seems incredible that powerful people once seized weaker people and kept them as possessions, to be work animals like livestock or sex servants like concubines. But it's a major part of history, dating back before the earliest written records. Slavery flowered through the Agricultural Age.

The Bible supported slavery. Leviticus 25 says: "Both thy bondmen, and thy bondmaids, which thou shalt have, shall be of the heathen that are round about you; of them shall ye buy bondmen and bondmaids…. And ye shall take them as an inheritance for your children after you, to inherit them for a possession; they shall be your bondmen forever."

In Exodus 21, the Bible even instructs Hebrews about selling their daughters into slavery.

Ancient Greece and Rome thrived on slave labor, with unpaid captives comprising perhaps one-fourth of the population. The word slave evidently derived from Slav, because multitudes of Slavs were seized by invaders and kept in bondage. Europe in the Dark Ages teemed with slavery. Russian serfs were slaves by a different name.

The story of abolition is a complex, tumultuous, liberal saga covering about ten centuries. Starting in the third century BCE, various Chinese and Indian rulers halted slavery, but their decrees later were reversed. From the 11th to 18th centuries, dozens of countries and city-states halted human enslavement -- often for the home state, while letting it continue in colonies. France abolished slavery in 1794, but Napoleon reinstated it in 1802. Britain mostly ceased holding slaves, but fought a long struggle over British ships that hauled chained Africans to the Americas.

In the United States, President Thomas Jefferson sent an 1806 message to Congress calling for criminalization of slave-dealers for "those violations of human rights... which the morality, the reputation and the best of our country have long been eager to proscribe."

The abolition movement snowballed across New England and northern states -- while the south remained a stubborn bastion of human slavery. Events and hostilities grew increasingly bitter and violent. Here's an example:

Thousands of rebellious southern slaves swam across rivers or fled into forests at night to escape through the Underground Railroad, in which sympathetic whites hid and fed them, then transported them north to free territory.

To halt this loss of southern property, Congress passed a new Fugitive Slave Act in 1850 requiring all federal officials to help capture runaways and send them back to slavery. Abolitionists called it the "Bloodhound Law" because dogs often were used to track the escapees.

In Syracuse, New York, some liberal-minded residents gathered in a protest group called the Liberty Party and vowed civil disobedience against the law. Leaders said they would hide fugitives in their own homes and fight federal agents, if necessary.

In 1851 a black Syracuse barrelmaker named Jerry McHenry was seized by marshals and dragged in manacles before a magistrate for extradition southward. He was painfully beaten. Liberty Party members rang church bells and summoned hundreds of protesters to jam the courtroom. Emotional chaos overwhelmed the proceeding, and white sympathizers rushed McHenry down a stairwell for a brief escape. Police soon caught him on a bridge with his helpers.

McHenry was locked in a police room with armed guards. Thousands of angry townspeople surrounded the courthouse and threw stones through windows. Hard-line Liberty Party members plotted a second escape. They didn't use guns, but employed a battering ram in the night to smash into the police quarters. Police panicked and shoved their prisoner out the door, into welcoming hands.

McHenry was spirited to hiding in sympathetic homes -- including the residence of a butcher who publicly denounced abolitionists, to deflect suspicion. The ex-slave secretly was treated by a doctor, and his chains were hammered off. Then he was dressed in female clothing and taken via the Underground Railroad to Lake Ontario, where a boat took him to slave-free Canada.

In the following decade before the Civil War erupted, no other fugitive slave was seized in the Syracuse area.

Here's another example:

Elijah Parish Lovejoy (1802-1837) was a Maine reformer who moved west and headed an anti-slavery newspaper, *The St. Louis Observer*. His writing infuriated pro-slavery residents, especially after he criticized a judge who failed to indict members of a mob who lynched a free black man. Three times, throngs of slavery supporters wrecked his press. Lovejoy gave a public speech saying he had broken no laws, but merely was expressing his beliefs as allowed by the Bill of Rights. He said he respected the views of slavery advocates, but felt he must challenge them. He vowed that he wouldn't be cowed into silence.

In 1837, he moved across the river into free-state Illinois and started the *Alton Observer*, hiding his new press in a warehouse and continuing his crusade. A pro-slavery mob tracked him down, stormed the warehouse, set if afire, and shot Lovejoy to death during a gunbattle.

Lovejoy became a martyr for the abolition cause. In an 1838 Lyceum address -- two decades before he became standard-bearer of the brand-new anti-slavery Republican Party -- Abraham Lincoln praised Lovejoy's memory. (My longtime newspaper publisher, W.E. "Ned" Chilton III, once received the Elijah Parish Lovejoy Award for selfless public crusades.)

Severe hatreds of the slavery era are clear in the tale of John Brown, who was

43

impelled by the Lovejoy murder to become an armed militant abolitionist. First, Brown helped runaway slaves escape northward through the Underground Railroad in New England. Then he and his sons moved in 1855 to Kansas, where near-warfare raged between slavery supporters and "free staters." The growing Brown group engaged in battles, and even hacked some slavery advocates to death with swords (to maintain nighttime silence and not rouse sleeping residents). Brown became wanted for murder, and returned east with his band of fighters.

Then Brown hatched a grand scheme to launch a national slave uprising. He planned to slip into the Potomac Valley, hide his squad in a rented farmhouse, then seize the federal armory at Harpers Ferry and use its weapons for a rebellion by slaves.

Escaped slave Frederick Douglass, who became a brilliant orator against slavery, secretly met Brown at an isolated stone quarry and tried to talk him out of armed action, but Brown was adamant.

All along, a clique of New England abolitionists, "the Secret Six," covertly funded Brown's crusade. The circle of wealthy and influential intellectuals even hid Brown in their homes while he was wanted for Kansas murders.   His clandestine backers were: Boston physician Samuel Howe, whose wife Julia Ward Howe wrote the *Battle Hymn of the Republic* -- Unitarian minister Theodore Parker, who called democracy "government of all the people, by all the people, for all the people," a phrase adapted famously by Lincoln --

millionaire abolitionist Gerrit Smith -- Harvard-educated thinker Franklin Sanborn, who taught Ralph Waldo Emerson's children -- philanthropist George Stearns -- and Unitarian preacher Thomas Higginson, editor of the *Atlantic Monthly*.

As everyone knows, Brown's plot failed. He seized the armory on Oct. 16, 1859, but slaves failed to join an insurrection. Brown's men were trapped and eventually executed.

Among the Secret Six backers, preacher Higginson was the fiercest radical. After Brown's capture, some other conspirators in the group fled to Canada to avoid arrest. Millionaire Smith denied involvement and committed himself to a mental asylum. Minister Parker stayed in Europe until his death. But Higginson defended Brown publicly -- and secretly plotted an armed attack to rescue Brown from his jail in what is now the Eastern Panhandle of West Virginia. Under heavy military guard, Brown was hanged before the rescue could occur.

Brown's bold raid electrified America, galvanizing both slavery defenders and slavery-haters. Polarization grew stronger. Emotions boiled until the pressure-cooker erupted into the ghastly Civil War, which killed more Americans (600,000-plus) than any other conflict.

Unitarian minister Higginson became a colonel in the Union Army and led a regiment of freed slaves in 1863 to capture Jacksonville, Florida. He hoped to trigger an insurrection by southern slaves, just as Brown had attempted at Harpers Ferry. But his attempt likewise failed.

The terrible curse of slavery finally was lifted from America, and the world. Slowly, nation after nation banned human bondage and seaborne slave trafficking. Colonial powers abandoned slavery in their colonies. Many Muslim countries halted it in the 1900s. The last place to outlaw it was Mauritania, in western North Africa, which criminalized slaveholding in 2007. The long eradication was a triumph of liberalism.

However, hidden from public view, various types of coerced labor and sexual bondage still occur around the world. In 1999, Anti-Slavery International estimated that 27 million people were trapped in unpaid servitude and forced labor.

Like most social struggles, the battle never is completely over.

Women's right to vote

Inferiority of females was presumed, and mandated, in virtually every human culture for millennia. Through most of history, the brawn of heavier males gave them dominance, and women held lesser status -- often mere possessions of men, like chattel, confined to the home, rarely educated, with few rights. Many were forced to wear veils or shrouds when outdoors, and they couldn't go outside without a male relative escort. Fathers kept their daughters restricted, then found husbands who became their new masters. Sometimes the husbands also had several other wives. In a few cultures, unwanted baby girls were left on trash dumps to die.

In the Bible, God told Eve: "I will greatly multiply thy sorrow and thy conception: in sorrow thou shalt bring forth children; and thy desire shall be to thy husband, and he shall rule over thee."

In a classic Euripides play in the fifth century BCE, Medea lamented: "Women would be better off as cattle than as we are, a subspecies of the human race. First, at great expense, we buy ourselves a husband. What is a dowry but a payment for marriage? But then he owns us, especially our bodies."

In a Sophocles play of the same era, Procne complained: "We women are nothing.... When we attain maidenhood, we are driven away from our homes, sold as merchandise, and compelled to marry. Some go to strange men's homes, others to foreigners, some to joyless houses, some to hostile. Once the first night has yoked us to our husbands, we are forced to praise him and say that all is well."

In Ancient Greece, women were kept indoors, rarely seen, while men performed all public functions. Women couldn't attend schools or own property. A wife couldn't attend male social events, even when her husband staged one at home. Aristotle believed in "natural slaves" and wrote that females are naturally inferior creatures who must be cared for, as a farmer tends his livestock. "In the same way, the relationship between the male and the female is by nature such that the male is higher, the female lower, that the male rules and the female is ruled."

Yet a peculiar thing happened: Greek male artists created thousands of sculptures and ceramic pictures of bold, strong, fighting, female Amazon warriors -- the opposite of Greek women. Evidently the Amazons were just a male fantasy. Perhaps psychiatrists can explain that odd phenomenon.

Up through medieval times, daughters were secondary, and inheritances went to firstborn sons. Male rule prevailed. Anthropologists have searched for exceptions, with little success -- except possibly some Iroquois tribes in Canada, where women reportedly had some rights. In the 1930s, Margaret Mead thought she found a female-led group in New Guinea, but she later reversed her conclusion and wrote: "All the claims so glibly made about societies ruled by women are nonsense. We have no reason to believe that they ever existed.... Men everywhere have been in charge of running the show."

As The Enlightenment blossomed in the 1700s, calls for women's rights emerged. France's Talleyrand wrote that only men required serious education -- "Men are destined to live on the stage of the world" -- and women should learn just to manage "the paternal home." This infuriated England's rebellious Mary Wollstonecraft (1759-1797), who wrote *A Vindication of the Rights of Woman*, contending that females have potential for full public life. (Her daughter married poet Percy Shelley and wrote *Frankenstein*.)

Reformer John Stuart Mill (1806-1873) wrote *The Subjugation of Women* in 1869, after his wife had written *The Enfranchisement of Women*, calling for a female right to vote. The husband protested: "There remain no legal slaves, save the mistress of every house." As a member of England's Parliament, Mill sought voting by women and became president of the National Society for Women's Suffrage.

"The legal subordination of one sex to another is wrong in itself, and now one of the chief hindrances to human improvement," Mill wrote, adding that since men have suffrage, "there is not a shadow of justification for not admitting women under the same."

All this was the background as the western world experienced a century-long liberal crusade that finally brought women the right to vote.

Elizabeth Cady Stanton (1815-1902) was the bright daughter of a New York state judge.

Few schools admitted girls, so her father arranged for her to attend male-only Johnstown Academy. The daughter grew outraged by laws forbidding women to own property or control their lives.

She married an abolitionist lawyer and accompanied him to London for a world conference against slavery. Women weren't allowed to participate; they sat silent behind a curtain while men spoke.

Back in America, she joined Quakers to organize an 1848 assembly at Seneca Falls, New York, that launched the modern women's equality movement. Frederick Douglass urged delegates to demand female suffrage. Stanton later joined Unitarians Susan B. Anthony, Lucy Stone and Ralph Waldo Emerson in a lifelong struggle for female rights.

The Civil War temporarily suppressed women's rights efforts, but they flared anew when the 15th Amendment, ratified in 1870, allowed black males to vote, but not females of any color. Demands snowballed for decades. Mark Twain gave a speech calling for female voting. Various suffrage groups took to the streets, some more militant than others. The National Woman's Party led by Alice Paul was toughest, picketing outside the White House, enduring male jeers and physical assaults.

President Woodrow Wilson tried to ignore the clamor. When a Russian delegation visited the White House, pickets held banners saying "America is not a democracy. Twenty million women are denied the right to vote." The protesters staged Washington parades that were attacked by mobs, sending some beaten victims to hospitals. Women pickets on sidewalks were hauled to jail on absurd charges of "obstructing traffic." When they refused to pay fines, they were locked up with criminals. Alice Paul was sentenced to seven months. She went on a hunger strike, and was force-fed.

Finally, Wilson reversed position in 1918 and supported female enfranchisement. Congress approved the 19th Amendment, and it was ratified in 1920, letting women vote.

As suffragette Lucy Stone lay dying in 1893, her final words to her daughter were: "Make the world better." That's the entire liberal message, summed up in four words.

The fact that many women's rights advocates also were abolitionists illustrates a psychological phenomenon: Liberal impulses usually cause people to support several unrelated progressive causes, a broad-spectrum left-wing agenda -- and conservative impulses similarly cause support for a group of allied right-wing issues.

One of my friends, a 90-year-old doctor, recalled that when she was a little girl, her suffragette mother took her to the White House and she sat on President Wilson's lap. One of my newspaper colleagues, Mary Walton, wrote a book subtitled *Alice Paul and the Battle for the Ballot.*

Around the world, various other nations allowed female voting, some more slowly than others. In Switzerland, women didn't gain full ballot rights in all districts until 1991. Saudi Arabian women finally gained only partial voting in December, 2015.

Social struggles never really end. Western women still haven't gained full equality. Their pay remains below the average for male workers. In some places, American women couldn't serve on juries until the 1950s. Some Muslim and African cultures remain medieval, with women subjugated, with girls less-educated, with "honor killings" of flirtatious daughters who besmirch a family's Puritanical standards, and with genital mutilation of girls to subdue their sex drive and keep them "pure" for husbands.

An Amnesty International report said:

"In the United States, a woman is raped every six minutes; a woman is battered every fifteen seconds. In North Africa, six thousand women are genitally mutilated each day. This year, more than fifteen thousand women will be sold into sexual slavery in China. Two hundred women in Bangladesh will be horribly disfigured when their spurned husbands or suitors burn them with acid. More than seven thousand women in India will be murdered by their families and in-laws in disputes over dowries. Violence against women is rooted in a global culture of discrimination which denies women equal rights with men and which legitimizes the appropriation of women's bodies for individual gratification or political ends. Every year, violence in the home and the community devastates the lives of millions of women."

Obviously, plenty of work remains for liberal reformers to do.

An early 'Occupy'

The terrible Great Depression of the 1930s wasn't America's only economic crash. Various lesser ones happened through the 1800s, almost in a twenty-year cycle, inflicting poverty and suffering on working-class families.

Especially severe was a collapse in the 1890s. Thousands of businesses went bankrupt. Hundreds of banks failed. Farmers couldn't find buyers for their crops. Around three million workers were jobless, roaming for charity, eating in soup kitchens and sleeping in shelters. In those times, America had no government safety net to help victims. The unlucky were cast into helplessness.

Amid the hardship, an Ohio reformer named Jacob Coxey hatched a dramatic plan: He called for an army of jobless men to march on Washington to demand federal work projects that would put the unemployed to work building roads, schools, libraries, hospitals, bridges and the like. He said his marchers would be a "petition in boots."

Coxey's right-hand man, Carl Browne, preached that the social gospel of Jesus demanded that America help miserable underdogs. He said all people have a share of Christ's soul inside them, so the populace should feel sympathy for the hungry and homeless. He and Coxey called their movement the Army of the Commonweal of Christ. A painting of Jesus was prepared for the marchers, and a commissary wagon was emblazoned, "Sell what you have and give to the poor."

Various out-of-work men and labor union members came to Coxey's home town of Massillon to join the proposed march. Conservative newspapers sent reporters who ridiculed the assemblage as "hoboes" and "dangerous cranks" in a "fanatical mob." Headlines derided "Coxey's Army."

The march began on Easter, 1894, along Ohio's crude and muddy roads. Some newspapers predicted that violence and criminality would result. But a strange thing happened: Sympathetic throngs greeted the band at each town, cheering the humanitarian cause, offering food, clothing and shelter to the hikers. One town contributed three hundred pairs of shoes. Others produced brass bands and picnic feasts.

Across Pennsylvania and Maryland, more jobless men joined the array, despite springtime cold, even snow. The parade grew to five hundred strong. At night, marchers huddled around campfires and slept in hay-filled barns.

As the march finally neared Washington, right-wing newspapers predicted armed violence and called for troops to quell the mob. But ten thousand Washingtonians turned out to greet and feed the visitors. Two thousand bicycle riders accompanied the procession. Four hundred Washington union members joined the throng.

Sympathetic congressmen introduced bills for federal work programs fitting Coxey's vision. Coxey demanded a right to speak at the Capitol, but police refused. Lines of officers blocked streets. During a confrontation, police clubbed some bystanders, while Coxey rushed to the Capitol steps to speak. Police subdued him -- but not before he handed his speech to a reporter.

Leaders of Coxey's Army were jailed on charges of walking on the Capitol lawn. Followers set up a campground to wait for Congress to act.

Meanwhile, copycat protest armies of jobless men formed around America and began heading for Washington. Some assembled in California, the Pacific Northwest, the Rockies, the Midwest and New England. Many rode freight trains to the nation's capital, where they joined the campers.

In the end, Congress didn't provide work relief. The encampment disintegrated in late summer. It was somewhat similar to the Occupy Wall Street episode that swept America in the early 21st century. Despite few tangible gains, it nonetheless focused a national spotlight on the plight of left-out people.

Free public schools

During the Agriculture Age, when most Americans worked with horse teams and plows, there was scant need for intellect and book knowledge. Many farm children were taught (a bit) at home, or attended one-room elementary schools where all ages sat together, learning simple spelling, reading and math. Some villages had "dame schools" in which women were paid (a bit) to teach children the alphabet and grammar around their fireplaces.

In colonial times, White Horse Taverns and Red Lion Inns had pictures of white horses and red lions, for the benefit of many who couldn't read writing on signs.

Two centuries ago, only affluent families could afford tutors or small private schools, such as the 1635 Boston Latin School. Blue-collar folks went untaught.

But the Industrial Revolution brought changing needs, and a movement for free public schools became a liberal quest.

Here's an example: Around 1800, some residents of Providence, Rhode Island, began a halting attempt to establish city schools for all. A barber asked the Mechanics Association, an assembly of many trades, to appeal to the state assembly for help. The association drafted a petition saying:

"The means of education enjoyed in this state are very inadequate to a purpose so highly important.... Members of the rising generation... are suffered to grow up in ignorance."

It asked for schools for all children, "and in particular those who are poor and destitute -- the son of the widow and child of distress."

Members wrote to newspapers demanding schools, because "genius is certainly to be found as well in the cottage as in the palace."

In Providence at that time, the only people eligible to vote were men owning at least $134 worth of real estate and the eldest sons of such property owners. Yet a Providence assembly voted in favor of public schools. In 1800, legislators approved the plan, and Rhode Island became America's first state with a law establishing statewide public schools.

Providence people raised money and opened schools attended by nearly a thousand boys and girls. Each student was required to pay for firewood.

In 1803, the state law was repealed -- but by then, public momentum for schools was snowballing.

Horace Mann (1796-1859) grew up in Puritanical Massachusetts, but he was repelled by hate-filled Calvinist preaching and joined the liberal Unitarian movement. He was elected to the legislature and clamored for abolition of slavery, asylums for the mentally ill, and especially free public schools with morality training but not sectarian religious indoctrination. He insisted on classes divided by age groups, with a standard curriculum used in all schools.

Mann -- an in-law of novelist Nathaniel Hawthorne -- was elected to Congress, succeeding the late John Quincy Adams. Later he became president of Antioch College in Ohio. His lifelong crusade for free public schools gave him the title "father of public education." While he pursued several liberal causes, he said: "Other reforms are remedial; education is preventative."

He told Antioch's 1859 graduating class: "Be ashamed to die until you have won some victory for humanity."

John Dewey (1859-1952) was another New England thinker and liberal reformer who championed free schooling. He became head of the philosophy department at the University of Chicago and spoke all over the world on the need for education.

State laws requiring compulsory school attendance began in the 1850s and slowly spread over America. The Progressive movement in the late 1800s pushed the effort. By the 1920s, one-third of American youths between age fourteen and seventeen attended high school.

Blacks were excluded from white schools until the blockbuster 1954 Supreme Court ruling that ordered integration. In the 1960s, federal money was funneled to state schools, and federal requirements imposed on them. In

1972, Congress passed Title IX giving girls equality in school athletics and other academic matters. Sexual harassment and discrimination against pregnant girls were outlawed.

As the world turns more high-tech in the snowballing Information Age, intense learning increasingly is crucial for modern careers. Free public education has become a pillar supporting society and the economy -- and giving everyone a chance for a future.

Birth control

Since early times, women attempted various folk remedies and other methods to avoid pregnancy. Some inserted moss, leaves, roots or crude cervical caps into themselves to block sperm. In ancient Greece and Rome, the silphium plant reportedly was ingested to induce abortion -- and over-harvesting perhaps helped cause the plant's extinction.

Effective birth control didn't become possible until the start of the 20th century, after vulcanization of rubber enabled workable diaphragms and condoms. Puritanical churches, especially Catholicism, denounced the development, saying it thwarted the will of God. Preventing pregnancy was equated with murder.

In Victorian Britain in the 1870s, radical reformers Annie Besant and Charles Bradlaugh edited the *National Reformer*, which championed trade unions, public education, woman's suffrage, workplace safety and birth control. They reprinted a forty-year-old pamphlet calling for contraception, and were arrested on charges of "obscene libel." They were acquitted, and their sensational trial helped erode prim sexual taboos.

In America, Margaret Sanger (1883-1966), spearheaded the birth control movement. Trained as a nurse, she worked in New York City tenements where she saw low-income women broken by endless childbearing. She recounted a 1912 incident in which a desperate mother nearly died from a self-induced abortion. The woman's doctor had no advice except to tell her husband to "sleep on the roof." When Sanger returned later, she found the woman pregnant again, and terminal.

Determined to combat unwanted pregnancy and venereal disease, Sanger went to Holland and learned of a new invention, the diaphragm. She returned to America and began publishing *The Woman Rebel*, which clamored for birth control. She was indicted under prudish Comstock laws.

In 1916, she opened America's first birth-control clinic, which was swiftly closed by police. Sanger was jailed thirty days for "maintaining a public nuisance." As she was booked into jail, she was asked her religion, and she replied, "Humanity." Altogether, the reformer was jailed eight times for mentioning sex.

In 1921, she founded the American Birth Control League, which later evolved into the Planned Parenthood Foundation. She was denounced incessantly by hidebound American ministers. In 1936, federal courts ruled that advocating contraception didn't violate Comstock laws. That same year, the American Medical Association revoked a former statement condemning birth control.

In 1965, a year before Sanger's death, America's Supreme Court scored a breakthrough in *Griswold v. Connecticut*, striking down state laws making it a crime to sell contraceptives to married couples.

Justices decreed that such couples have a right of privacy in their bedrooms. In 1972, a follow-up case, *Eisenstadt v. Baird*, extended the right to unwed couples.

Legalization of birth control was another triumph for liberalism. Slowly, western civilization began to consider avoidance of pregnancy a human right.

In 2010, President Barack Obama's landmark Affordable Care Act, extending medical insurance to millions of lower-income Americans, provided that all health plans (except those of churches) must provide contraception to women employees at no cost. Republicans and conservative denominations exploded in protest. They filed several lawsuits contending that "religious freedom" should allow devout employers to deny birth control to their female workers. Republicans in Congress pushed legislation to guarantee this freedom for employers. The Supreme Court allowed a tiny fringe of firms and religious entities to elude the mandate, but the vast majority of America welcomed it.

Progressives mostly have won the battle for birth control, although a few pockets of resistance remain.

Progressive Party

Strangely, America's two major political parties gradually reversed identities, like the magnetic poles of Planet Earth switching direction.

When the Republican Party was formed in 1856, it was fiercely liberal, opposing the expansion of slavery, calling for more spending on public education, seeking more open immigration, and the like. Compassionate Abraham Lincoln suited the new party's progressive agenda.

In that era, Democrats were conservatives, partly dominated by the slaveholding South. Those old-style Democrats generally opposed any government action to create jobs or help underdogs.

Through the latter half of the 19th century, the pattern of Republicans as liberals, Democrats as conservatives, generally held true. In 1888, the GOP elected President Benjamin Harrison (1833-1901) on a liberal platform seeking more social services.

Then in 1896, a reversal began when Democrats nominated populist firebrand William Jennings Bryan (1860-1925), "the Great Commoner."

"He was the first liberal to win the Democratic Party presidential nomination," political scholar Rich Rubino wrote. "This represented a radical departure from the conservative roots of the Democratic Party."

Meanwhile, the GOP began shifting to conservative. Theodore Roosevelt (1858-1919) -- a vice president who took the top office after William McKinley was assassinated in 1901 -- was a Republican liberal who supported a "Square Deal" for working families. He broke up monopolistic trusts of rich corporations. He championed pure food and drugs. He created national parks and forests for the enjoyment of everyone. He won the 1906 Nobel Peace Prize for helping end war between Russia and Japan.

After leaving office, Roosevelt felt that his successor, William Howard Taft (1857-1930), was leading America too far to the right. So T.R. challenged Taft for the GOP nomination in 1912, and lost. In rebellion, Roosevelt gathered his liberal delegates and formed the Progressive Party, with a bold platform bordering on socialism.

The new-formed party called for universal medical care under a National Health Service. It sought government pensions for retirees, plus compensation for the jobless and disabled. It demanded an eight-hour workday, and a minimum wage for women. It sought a constitutional amendment to allow a federal income tax. It supported voting by women, more freedom for workers to organize and strike, inheritance tax on rich estates, worker's compensation for on-the-job injuries, and many other left-wing goals.

The Progressive platform attacked big-money influence in politics, vowing "to destroy this invisible government, to dissolve the unholy alliance between corrupt business and corrupt politics."

Roosevelt was a fiery orator and writer, saying: "I believe that there should be a very much heavier progressive tax on very large incomes, a tax which should increase in a very marked fashion for the gigantic incomes."

"The supreme duty of the nation is the conservation of human resources through an enlightened measure of social and industrial justice. We pledge ourselves to work unceasingly in state and nation for... the protection of home life against the hazards of sickness, irregular employment and old age through the adoption of a system of social insurance adapted to American use."

"It is essential that there should be organization of labor. This is an era of organization. Capital organizes and therefore labor must organize."

While Roosevelt was campaigning in Milwaukee in 1912, a crazed assassin, John Schrank -- who claimed that the ghost of William McKinley asked him to avenge McKinley's death by killing Roosevelt -- shot the Progressive candidate in the chest. The bullet was partly deflected by Roosevelt's fifty-page speech and his steel eyeglasses case, but wounded him nonetheless. Bleeding, he continued to orate unfazed.

Later, when reporters asked if the wounding would deter his campaign, Roosevelt replied that he was "fit as a bull moose." Thereafter, his party was dubbed the Bull Moose Party.

Progressives won about one-fourth of the 1912 popular vote, and Democrat Woodrow Wilson (1856-1924) attained the presidency. In 1916, Roosevelt declined the Progressive nomination, and the liberal party he created soon disintegrated.

Ensuing decades saw Republicans grow steadily more conservative, and Democrats acquire the liberal mantle. When the Great Depression struck, the "New Deal" of Democrat Franklin Delano Roosevelt (1882-1945), Theodore's nephew-in-law, achieved landmark progressive reforms. In the 1960s, the "Great Society" of Democrat Lyndon Johnson (1908-1973) vastly expanded the public safety net and gave legal equality to African Americans -- driving racist Dixie out of the Democratic Party, into the GOP. Then Republican President Ronald Reagan (1911-2004) mobilized the "religious right" of white evangelicals for his party. Later, extreme white conservatives calling themselves "Tea Party" militants emerged in the GOP.

All this outlines America's political flipflop -- how the liberal Republican Party turned conservative, and the conservative Democratic Party turned liberal. It was a fascinating transition.

Deadly labor struggles

As the Industrial Revolution snowballed, millions of workmen left farms and took urban factory jobs to support their families. Society was transformed. Mass blue-collar workforces grew -- but workers often were subjected to exhausting hours, low pay and unhealthy conditions. Their misery spawned an urge to organize for self-protection.

Here's a historic example:

In the 1830s, coal-loaders on Philadelphia's waterfront were forced to work sixteen hours a day, six days a week. They staggered to their slum homes at night, black from coal dust, almost too weary to wash or enjoy their families, only to return before daylight for another sixteen hours.

One day, the embittered men abruptly walked off the job and demanded a ten-hour workday. It was a jolt that idled much of the ship wharves. Coal merchants rejected their demand and vowed to hire replacement workers. Some newspapers called the strikers "deluded" and even "freshly imported foreigners who despise and defy the law."

Then Philadelphia's handloom weavers decided that they, too, should have their work hours reduced to ten per day. They likewise struck. Next, cordwainers (shoemakers) joined the demand. At a rally, speakers denounced the "grinding avarice" of shoe company owners and vowed that cordwainers would no longer be "slaves of heartless monopolists."

Strikers marched through streets and stormed into the Merchants Exchange. A leader rebuked the "blood-sucking aristocracy" that kept workers subjugated. They wrote a resolution declaring:

"As we have nothing to dispose of but our labor, we claim the right of freemen of selling that at such a price as shall enable us to support ourselves, our wives and our families, without becoming objects of public charity."

Journeymen carpenters, bricklayers, housepainters, plasterers, ironsmiths and tinsmiths joined the walkout for ten-hour days. Thousands of people signed a petition to Philadelphia's council, which decreed that all city employees would work shorter hours. Philadelphia became the first city in America to shorten the workday for its workers.

Workers wrote more resolutions declaring that opponents of the ten-hour day were "devoid of the noble principle of humanity and the mild and charitable virtues of Christianity." They called the city's working conditions "an odious system of oppression." They said employers "hold us as slaves."

Slowly, business after business capitulated to the demands, and the ten-hour workday became standard. The Philadelphia victory helped spur rapid growth of organized unions around America.

Meanwhile, gory violence accompanied unionization in some parts of America. My state of West Virginia was a battleground where coal miners were exploited like cattle, and many fought back in armed uprisings. The West Virginia mine wars were legendary. Here's a brief record:

As coal mining blossomed in the late 1800s, thousands of immigrants and blacks poured into southern West Virginia for dirty, dangerous coal jobs. The diggers mostly lived in company camps, were paid in "scrip" tokens spendable only at company stores, and were exploited somewhat like serfs in bondage. Explosions and cave-ins killed multitudes. In 1907, a mine blast at Monongah, West Virginia, took nearly 400 worker lives. One historian said American combat troops in World War I had better survival rates than West Virginia miners.

Appalachian Heritage magazine told how a large coal company store at Whipple, Fayette County, was a fortress for armed guards, a mortuary for killed miners, a citadel for subjugating miner families, a place where any gossip about union organizing led to swift dismissal -- and even a place where some desperate miner wives were coerced to trade sex for food for their hungry families.

After the store was abandoned, a purchaser found it contained odd, half-size lunchpails. Old-timers explained: When a miner was killed on the job, his wife and children soon were evicted from company-owned housing -- unless the widow sent a young son, perhaps eight, to become an apprentice digger in the late father's place. The small pails were for child miners.

In company housing around the store, mine owners arranged an ethnic mix of black miners, local Appalachian whites and imported Poles and other foreign-speaking immigrants -- to prevent workers from associating and trying to form a union. Assemblies by miners were forbidden.

As the stormy labor-organizing movement grew, disguised Baldwin-Felts guards were planted as supposed clerks in the Whipple store to listen for hints of union talk. Others were sent into mines posing as diggers for the same purpose. Any miner who "talked union" was fired and his family evicted. Mining in the early 1900s was extremely dangerous. The Whipple store had an embalming room in the basement for accident victims, and a special floor for coffins.

A secluded upstairs chamber was called the "rape room" by oldsters. If a miner's wife or teen-age daughter couldn't afford shoes, she was taken there by a guard who demanded that she earn them in bed. Miners were paid in company-issued "scrip" tokens redeemable at the store. But there also was a special paper scrip which some miner wives called "Esau" after the Bible's story of a starving elder son who sold his birthright to a younger brother for food. The paper scrip worked like this:

If a miner became injured or sick and couldn't go into the mines, his family soon ran out of food and became desperate. If his wife begged for rations at the Whipple store, she was issued the paper credit -- on agreement that she would repay later in cash or in sexual favors for guards and supervisors. She didn't dare tell her husband, and often tried to avoid the sexual payback.

As West Virginia's historic mine wars erupted, the Whipple store increasingly was headquarters for armed Baldwin-Felts agents trying to block unionization.

The mine wars were America's worst conflict since the Civil War, and the worst labor violence in American history. They involved the Army and military aircraft, plus civilian planes dropping homemade bombs. The new-formed United Mine Workers attempted to unionize diggers, which brought fierce resistance. Mine owners hired armed guards. Brutality abounded. Union organizers -- including tough-talking Mary "Mother" Jones -- were jailed repeatedly in West Virginia.

Mother Jones was a firebrand who proclaimed "Pray for the dead and fight like hell for the living." Upton Sinclair said she traveled around America, spurring various strikers in "a veritable odyssey of revolt."

In 1912, Paint Creek miners east of Charleston went on strike. Forced out of their company homes, they lived in tent clusters. To counter armed company guards, the UMW sent in guns and ammunition. Gov. William Glasscock declared martial law. A coal operator put machine guns on a train dubbed "the Bull Moose Special" which rolled along Paint Creek in 1913 firing at tents. Only one striker was killed -- reportedly because armored slits in the train cars prevented the machine guns from tilting downward toward crouching, hiding targets. In retaliation, armed miners attacked a nearby guard camp in a battle that killed sixteen.

By 1919, southern counties were a major nonunion zone. Mine owners paid Logan County Sheriff Don Chafin -- a political dictator who controlled every public job in the county -- to hire many "deputies" to beat and expel union agents and miners who attended organizing sessions. Chafin's sheriff salary was $3,500 a year, but a later inquiry learned that mine owners paid him about $33,000 more annually. He grew rich, and brutal. He was shot twice in clashes with miners.

In 1919, armed miners assembled near Charleston to march on Logan. They wore red bandannas and called themselves "rednecks." They made it halfway, but turned back.

In 1920, Mingo County miners struck. Armed Baldwin-Felts agents evicted them from company houses. Matewan Police Chief Sid Hatfield backed the strikers. He led a squad of armed miners to face the union-busters at the town's railway platform. The shootout killed seven guards and four townspeople, including the town mayor. Hatfield soon married the mayor's widow.

Near-warfare ensued in Mingo. In 1921, a three-day gunbattle raged, killing perhaps twenty. President Warren Harding declared martial law in West Virginia. Gov. Ephriam Morgan proclaimed that the region was in "a state of war, insurrection and riot." West

Virginia's State Police force was created chiefly to curb coalfield violence.

Police Chief Hatfield, ruled innocent in the "Matewan Massacre," was charged with a different shooting at a coal camp in adjoining McDowell County, along with a companion. As the two walked up the steps of the McDowell courthouse at Welch for a hearing, Baldwin-Felts men in the crowd stepped out and shot them both to death.

The Hatfield murder inflamed union miners. They rallied at the Capitol in Charleston and vowed to march southward like an army. UMW leaders roused workers to arm themselves. In Logan County, Sheriff Chafin had been preparing for such an invasion. He enlarged his deputy legion to around seven hundred, brought in machine guns, and built war-style breastworks on Blair Mountain, a natural barrier shielding the county seat of Logan. Chafin also engaged his own air force: three rented biplanes to scout for approaching mobs and drop homemade bombs on them.

About 5,000 bandanna-wearing "rednecks" gathered and headed south on Aug. 24, 1921. More joined them along the way, swelling the throng to an estimated 10,000 to 15,000. As the first groups approached Blair Mountain, some strikers hijacked a train and backed it fifteen miles to transport fighters.

Among the rebels was Baptist minister James Wilburn, who mobilized a squad of armed supporters. On Aug. 31, Wilburn's men killed three of Chafin's deputies, and one of the preacher's fighters died.

Full-scale warfare between defenders atop Blair and strikers below ensued for several days. Chafin's forces included state troopers, militiamen, Baldwin-Felts guards and deputized Logan countians. Hundreds of thousands of bullets were fired in the woodland, but casualties were surprisingly light, perhaps under twenty. Nobody knows an accurate body count.

President Harding sent federal troops from Kentucky, plus an air squadron under war hero Billy Mitchell from Langley Field near Washington. Mitchell's biplanes landed in an open field near Charleston -- but six got lost and crashed in mountains en route.

Rather than fight the Army, strikers withdrew. Many hid their guns in the woods, took off their red bandannas, and slipped away.

After the Battle of Blair Mountain, grand juries returned 1,217 indictments, including 325 for murder and twenty-four for treason. But the charges mostly evaporated. The only treason conviction was against a Walter Allen, who skipped bail and vanished, never to be found. Bill Blizzard, the "general" of the miner army, was tried in the same Jefferson County Courthouse where John Brown had been convicted of treason in 1859. Unlike Brown, Blizzard was cleared. Preacher Wilburn and his son were convicted of murder, but Gov. Howard Gore pardoned them after they served three years in prison.

The mine wars wiped out most of the UMW's funds and left it weak. By 1924, it had lost about half of its West Virginia members. Unions remained under severe attack until 1933, when President Roosevelt's New Deal legalized the right of workers to organize. March leader Blizzard, revered among miners, became UMW district president and led rapid unionization of the Mountain State.

Around America, various other violent conflicts and massacres accompanied the growth of labor unions. The right of workers to seek better conditions slowly won the eight-hour workday, the five-day workweek, a minimum wage, abolition of child labor and many other benefits. Support of unions became a bedrock principle of liberal politics.

"What does labor want? We want more schoolhouses and less jails, more books and less arsenals, more learning and less vice, more leisure and less greed, more justice and less revenge," said American Federation of Labor founder Samuel Gompers (1850-1924).

President Jimmy Carter said: "Every advance in this half-century -- Social Security, civil rights, Medicare, aid to education, one after another -- came with the support and leadership of American labor."

Abolitionist Wendell Phillips (1811-1884) said: "The labor movement means just this: It is the last noble protest of the American people against the power of incorporated wealth."

In a 1961 essay titled *If the Negro Wins, Labor Wins*, Dr. Martin Luther King Jr. (1929-1968) wrote: "Our needs are identical to labor's needs: decent wages, fair working conditions, livable housing, old-age security, health and welfare measures.... That is why the labor-hater and labor-baiter is virtually always a two-headed creature spewing anti-Negro epithets from one mouth and anti-labor propaganda from the other mouth."

But trends of economics and technology slowly undercut the union movement. As jobs grew more specialized and individualized -- and machines took over many tasks -- the need for blue-collar armies shrank. Unions were squeezed to the sidelines.

In the 1950s, when American manufacturing boomed, about one-third of all workers carried union cards. But steady erosion occurred. Today, only 6.7 percent of private-sector workers are union members. However, white-collar government jobs remain one-third unionized.

Republican legislators work incessantly to destroy unions. Right-to-work laws -- designed to break unions by letting some employees refuse to join locals and also refuse to contribute payments for collective bargaining -- have been passed in half of American states.

The retreat of unions is among a few sectors in which conservatives have scored greater success than progressives.

The New Deal

A golden age of liberalism arose in the 1930s as President Franklin Delano Roosevelt and his "New Deal" rescued America from the Great Depression. That tumultuous era launched the public safety net to protect families from agonies of life.

Previously, Americans had no safeguards against poverty, job loss, old-age deprivation, disabilities, bank failures, stock scams and other ills. They were defenseless against painful hardships. At that time, the United States was the only modern democracy without any social protections.

After the historic stock market crash in 1929, calamity snowballed. Millions of investors were wiped out. Nearly half of American banks failed. Around fourteen million workers -- nearly one-fourth of the total at that time -- lost employment. Many who stayed employed suffered pay cuts. Nearly a million mortgages were foreclosed. Jobless throngs roamed in search of charity. Homelessness became a crisis. Emergency soup kitchens and food pantries helped many survive.

Amid the suffering, some leaders feared insurrection. The most radical labor group in the early 1900s was the communistic Industrial Workers of the World, the "Wobblies," whose constitution began:

"The working class and the employing class have nothing in common. There can be no peace so long as hunger and want are found among millions of the working people, and the few who make up the employing class have all the good things of life."

Wobblies gathered and sang (to the tune of *The Sweet Bye and Bye*):

"Long-haired-preachers come out every night, and they tell us what's wrong and what's right -- but when asked about something to eat, they reply in a chorus so sweet: You will eat, bye and bye, in that beautiful home in the sky (way up high). Work and pray, live on hay -- you'll get pie in the sky when you die (that's a lie)."

The Republican administration of President Herbert Hoover floundered helplessly amid the economic collapse. But Democratic challenger Roosevelt promised a rescue, and was elected overwhelmingly. After he took office in 1933, the government plunged into mammoth liberal reforms.

Roosevelt's labor secretary, Frances Perkins -- a driving force of the New Deal -- drafted a set of goals for America, as outlined in her biography: "A forty-hour work week, a minimum wage, worker's compensation [for on-the-job injuries], a federal law banning child labor, direct federal aid for unemployment relief, Social Security, a revitalized public employment service, and health insurance."

Achievements under FDR transformed America:

Social Security gave pensions to the aged and disabled.

The Civilian Conservation Corps put three million jobless young men to work in camps building eight hundred parks, planting three billion trees, constructing remote roads and buildings, and other tasks.

The Public Works Administration, followed by the Works Progress Administration, hired millions more to build dams, highways, bridges, tunnels, airports, hospitals, schools, public housing, Navy ships, courthouses, city streets, electrical projects, and the like.

Unemployment compensation helped laid-off workers.

Workers compensation helped injured workers.

The Federal Deposit Insurance Corporation insured bank deposits up to $2,500, for the first time saving people from loss when banks failed.

The Securities Exchange Commission was created to prevent stock abuses of the sort that helped cause the Great Depression.

Food stamps helped needy families buy groceries.

Welfare "relief" aided those in deepest poverty.

The Tennessee Valley Authority created hydroelectric dams and supplied electricity to a wide region.

The only safety net goal envisioned by Secretary Perkins that failed to materialize was health insurance. (That breakthrough came later when the "Great Society" of Democratic

President Lyndon Johnson created Medicare and Medicaid in the 1960s.)

Roosevelt gave "fireside chat" radio talks to reassure troubled Americans. His was a noble voice for liberalism. In his 1934 message to Congress, he said:

"These three great objectives -- security of the home, security of livelihood and security of social insurance -- are, it seems to me, a minimum of the promise that we can offer to the American people. They constitute a right which belongs to every individual and every family willing to work."

Other FDR comments:

"The test of our progress is not whether we add more to the abundance of those who have much; it is whether we provide enough for those who have little."

"In our personal ambitions we are individualists. But in our seeking for economic and political progress as a nation, we all go up or else all go down as one people."

"The liberty of a democracy is not safe if the people tolerate the growth of private power to a point where it becomes stronger than their democratic state itself. That, in its essence, is fascism - ownership of government by an individual, by a group."

"A conservative is a man with two perfectly good legs who, however, has never learned to walk forward."

"A nation that destroys its soils destroys itself. Forests are the lungs of our land, purifying the air and giving fresh strength to our people."

"Human kindness has never weakened the stamina or softened the fiber of a free people. A nation does not have to be cruel to be tough."

"Taxes, after all, are dues that we pay for the privileges of membership in an organized society."

"The Social Security Act offers to all our citizens a workable and working method of meeting urgent present needs and of forestalling future need. It utilizes the familiar machinery of our federal-state government to promote the common welfare and the economic stability of the nation."

"No business which depends for existence on paying less than living wages to its workers has any right to continue in this country. By living wages I mean more than a bare subsistence level - I mean the wages of decent living."

"Not only our future economic soundness but the very soundness of our democratic institutions depends on the determination of our government to give employment to idle men."

Roosevelt was hated and denounced endlessly by many conservatives. A few allegedly plotted to overthrow him and seize the government. Here's an account:

Marine Corps General Smedley Butler was America's most-decorated hero, who fought in World War I, the Philippines, China and other theaters. He received the

Congressional Medal of Honor twice. Veterans admired him.

In 1934, the retired general testified before Congress that a clique of Wall Street financiers secretly tried to recruit him into a sinister plot to topple FDR. According to the scheme, he was to lead thousands of jobless veterans in a massive Washington rally, then surround the White House and occupy it to remove the president -- much as fascists in Italy had seized control and put Benito Mussolini into power. Instead of cooperating with the planned coup, Butler exposed it.

One report said Roosevelt might have prosecuted the Wall Street clique for treason, but instead struck a bargain to help America: If the plotters ended their opposition and let Congress pass Social Security, FDR's Justice Department wouldn't press treason charges.

Footnote: Many years ago, I took a break from my long newspaper career and served briefly in Washington as press secretary to Sen. Robert C. Byrd, Democrat of West Virginia.

His fellow Mountain State senator, also a Democrat, was Jennings Randolph, a courtly oldster who first was elected to Congress in 1932 as part of Roosevelt's New Deal crusade. Randolph kept a small note on his desk saying:

"The most important lesson you can learn in life is that other people are as real behind their eyes as you are behind yours."

That little note conveyed a truth of liberalism.

Racial equality

When I came of age in the 1950s, African Americans were shunned outcasts, treated as tainted inferiors, denied the privileges and benefits of white society. They were forced to live in squalid ghettos, like Indians on reservations. They were rejected for good white jobs, even if they held college degrees. They couldn't enter white restaurants, white theaters, white hotels, white swimming pools, etc. (except to work as low-paid maids, janitors and the like). Their children couldn't enter white schools, but were sent to inferior black schools. White police constantly stormed black zones, kicking in doors in liquor and prostitution raids, but rarely treated white zones in that manner. In Dixie, cruel lynchings lingered.

When the historic civil rights movement stirred, my Unitarian congregation was fiercely involved. Members joined sit-ins at lunch counters refusing to serve blacks. Members joined equality marches. They clamored for human rights laws and joined integration committees. They even helped create a mixed-race day-care center in a poor African American ghetto. My pre-school children attended it. I was swept up in the crusade against Jim Crow segregation. I made a one-person attempt to integrate the members-only lake community where I lived outside Charleston, West Virginia.

Likewise, my left-leaning newspaper, *The Charleston Gazette*, the state's largest, pounded drums for integration. Publisher Ned Chilton and his wife Betty fought hard against the old apartheid.

I was elated when the long, painful, historic civil rights struggle attained victory. As a naïve young idealist, I thought that blacks finally -- free from centuries of oppression -- would move into America's middle class, earn college degrees, enter desirable careers and raise secure families.

But a disappointment happened: After integration succeeded, it gradually became clear that poverty, crime, drugs, hidden prejudice and other social blights still cursed much of the African American community. De-facto segregation still excluded many blacks from good jobs and opportunities. While a few educated blacks moved upward, the wonderful civil rights victory failed to produce the glorious transformation I had envisioned. In fact, as successful blacks were allowed to move out of ghettos, the loss of natural leaders left their old neighborhoods more vulnerable to degradation. A lesson was clear: Societal struggles are much more complex and difficult than they seem at first glance.

Nonetheless, America's legendary civil rights movement was a progressive triumph of enormous proportions. It belongs in a Liberal Hall of Fame. It wiped out entrenched apartheid that conservatives had defended for a century. Here's a partial chronicle:

Thurgood Marshall (1908-1993) grew up in Baltimore, grandson of a slave. After college, he wanted to attend the University of Maryland law school, but it wouldn't admit blacks, so he graduated at the top of his class at Howard University.

After becoming an NAACP attorney, Marshall won impressive Supreme Court victories. In 1944, he wiped out all-white Democratic Party primary elections in Texas. In 1948, he defeated white-only covenants in property deeds. In 1950, he forced the University of Texas law school to integrate. And in 1954 came the blockbuster that changed America forever: *Brown v. Board of Education*, which forced public schools to integrate.

To the outrage of southern racists, President Kennedy appointed Marshall a federal appeals judge, then President Johnson named him America's solicitor general. Then came a breakthrough nomination to the Supreme Court. One of my newspaper colleagues, Wil Haygood, outlined this episode in a book titled *Showdown: Thurgood Marshall and the Supreme Court Nomination that Changed America.*

Haygood said LBJ's desire to make Marshall the nation's first black Supreme Court justice faced a problem: no vacancy. So the crafty Johnson pulled a scheme: He told aging Justice Tom Clark that he would appoint his son Ramsey as attorney general, but it would be awkward with his father on the high court. So the elder Clark retired, his son became attorney general, and Marshall was appointed to the new Supreme Court vacancy.

Angry southern senators vowed to filibuster and block the nominee. They stalled a hearing on him -- but racial rioting exploded in Detroit over police killings of unarmed black youths, putting pressure on the Senate to act. Then Johnson pulled another manipulation: "The cunning LBJ persuaded twenty segregationist senators to abstain from voting, an unbelievable occurrence for such a charged and historic vote," Haygood wrote.

Marshall's nomination was confirmed in 1967, and he became the first black justice on the nation's highest court since it was founded in 1789.

"Marshall wrote 322 majority opinions while on the high court," Haygood wrote. "They [ranged] from freedom of speech to the death penalty, from issues of segregation and discrimination to housing. There were also 363 dissents, giving evidence of a justice who would not bend when he felt the law was against the aggrieved and the dispossessed."

Haygood added: "President Johnson had signed the 1964 Civil Rights Act and 1965 Voting Rights Act, and the nomination of Marshall was the final nail in the coffin of white supremacy. There was this great drama taking place in the White House against the backdrop of riots and protests."

Nearly all Americans know the rest of the black equality story: Here's a major milestone:

In Montgomery, Alabama, blacks were required to get on the front of city buses to pay fares, then exit and reboard through a rear door to sit in back seats. If too many whites boarded front seats, drivers moved white-only dividers backward, forcing some blacks to surrender their seats. One day in 1955, Rosa Parks, sitting in the rear, stubbornly refused to give her seat to a white, calling it unfair. She was arrested.

Her arrest was like a small crack that burst a dam, loosing a flood of pent-up African American frustration. Black leaders organized resistance and named a local Baptist minister, Dr. Martin Luther King Jr., as their chief. They staged a boycott of Montgomery buses that ensued for a year, nearly bankrupting the bus system. White racists retaliated, burning black churches and bombing the homes of Dr. King and another black leader.

In 1956, courts ruled bus segregation illegal. A landmark liberal victory was attained.

Meanwhile, Rosa Parks and her husband both were fired from their jobs, and moved to Detroit. She landed a job on the staff of Rep. John Conyers, Democrat of Michigan. As her fame grew, she was named to the board of the Planned Parenthood Federation of America. She established a foundation that ran "Pathways to Freedom" bus tours of civil rights and Underground Railroad sites. She wrote books about her experience. In 1996, Bill Clinton gave her the Presidential Medal of Freedom. The following year, she was awarded the Congressional Gold Medal. In 1999, *Time* magazine named her among "the twenty most influential people of the twentieth century."

When she died in 2005 at age 92, her body lay in state at the Capitol rotunda in Washington, where 50,000 mourners passed. The U.S. Postal Service issued a stamp bearing her portrait. In 2013, President Obama unveiled her statue in the Capitol and said: "In a single moment, with the simplest of gestures, she helped change America and change the world."

Dr. Martin Luther King Jr. is a towering symbol known to every American. After leading the Montgomery bus boycott, he spent the rest of his brief life in a heroic, nonviolent crusade that gradually wiped out America's racial segregation and guaranteed black equality. He won the Nobel Peace Prize for his selfless sacrifice. King was martyred by a white assassin. Now a national holiday is held in his honor, and a major monument in Washington preserves his memory. He's a worldwide hero.

Few people know that King and his wife Coretta, although commonly identified as deep-south Baptists, began their adult lives in Boston attending off-brand Unitarian churches that doubt the divinity of Christ. Coretta later recounted that they decided to move into the heart of segregation in Dixie because it presented the best opportunity to work for racial improvement.

Later, when King declared that "the arc of the moral universe is long, but it bends toward justice," he was paraphrasing radical

Unitarian minister Theodore Parker (1810-1860), a fiery Trancendentalist, abolitionist and religious renegade.

What distinguished King was his amazing eloquence that swayed everyone who heard him. His appeals for decency and justice were heart-touching.

Amid the chaos of the bus boycott in 1955, he told supporters: "If you will protest courageously, and yet with dignity and Christian love, when the history books are written in future generations, the historians will have to pause and say, 'There lived a great people -- a black people -- who injected new meaning and dignity into the veins of civilization.'"

Writing in *The Wall Street Journal* in 1962, King said: "It may be true that the law cannot make a man love me, but it can keep him from lynching me, and I think that's pretty important."

After the Supreme Court banned government-led school prayer in 1962, King called it "a sound and good decision reaffirming something that is basic in our constitution: namely, separation of church and state."

The Council for Secular Humanism quoted King: "The hope of the world is still in dedicated minorities. The trailblazers in human, academic, scientific and religious freedom have always been in the minority."

While he was locked in a Birmingham jail in 1963 -- and many white, liberal, American ministers waffled about supporting the black equality movement -- he wrote: "Shallow understanding from people of good will is more frustrating than absolute misunderstanding from people of ill will."

After his jailing, he wrote an essay titled *Why We Can't Wait* , saying:

"I submit that an individual who breaks a law that conscience tells him is unjust, and who willingly accepts the penalty of imprisonment in order to rouse the conscience of the community over its injustice, is in reality expressing the higher respect for the law…. Non-violence is a powerful and just weapon... which cuts without wounding and ennobles the man who wields it. It is a sword that heals."

Famously, in his address at the Lincoln Memorial during a 1963 march on Washington, he said:

"I have a dream that one day on the red hills of Georgia, the sons of former slaves and the sons of former slaveowners will be able to sit together at the table of brotherhood.... I have a dream that my four little children will one day live in a nation where they will not be judged by the color of their skin, but by the content of their character."

Later in 1963, he said in a Birmingham speech: "Before the Pilgrims landed at Plymouth, we were here. Before the pen of Jefferson etched across the pages of history the majestic words of the Declaration of Independence, we were here. If the inexpressible cruelties of slavery could not stop us, the opposition we now face will surely fail…. A riot is the language of the unheard."

In his Nobel acceptance speech in 1964, he said:

"I have the audacity to believe that peoples everywhere can have three meals a day for their bodies, education and culture for their minds, and dignity, equality and freedom for their spirits. I believe that what self-centered men have torn down, men other-centered can build up.... I believe that unarmed truth and unconditional love will have the final word in reality. This is why right, temporarily defeated, is stronger than evil triumphant."

After he received death threats in 1964, King said in a speech at St. Augustine, Florida: "If physical death is the price that I must pay to free my white brothers and sisters from a permanent death of the spirit, then nothing can be more redemptive."

In *Ebony* magazine in 1965, he wrote: "Darkness cannot drive out darkness; only light can do that. Hate cannot drive out hate; only love can do that."

In a 1967 address to the Southern Christian Leadership Conference at Atlanta, King said: "Discrimination is a hellhound that gnaws at Negroes in every waking moment of their lives to remind them that the lie of their inferiority is accepted as truth in the society dominating them.... It is incontestable and deplorable that Negroes have committed crimes; but they are derivative crimes. They are born of the greater crimes of white society."

In a 1967 essay titled *Where Do We Go From Here*, he wrote: "The ultimate weakness of violence is that it is a descending spiral, begetting the very thing it seeks to destroy. Instead of diminishing evil, it multiplies it.... Violence merely increases hate."

As an opponent of the Vietnam War, King said in a 1967 sermon at Riverside Church in New York City:

"Somehow this madness must cease. I speak for those whose land is being laid waste, whose homes are being destroyed, whose culture is being subverted. I speak for the poor of America who are paying the double price of smashed hopes at home and death and corruption in Vietnam. The great initiative in this war is ours. The initiative to stop it must be ours."

On April 3, 1968, the night before his assassination, King said in Memphis:

"I've looked over, and I've seen the promised land. I may not get there with you, but I want you to know tonight that we as a people will get to the promised land.... So I'm happy tonight. I'm not worried about anything. I'm not fearing any man. Mine eyes have seen the glory of the coming of the Lord."

The great civil rights movement a half-century ago has entered history as a triumph of liberalism. It improved America forever. It cannot be undone.

'Dislodge traitors'

The Cold War fixated much of humanity for nearly half a century. After World War II, Russian communism took control of Eastern Europe, and Asian communists seized China, North Korea and North Vietnam. Western capitalism was alarmed. Constant conflict grew between capitalist democracies and totalitarian communism.

Fear of leftists became an American obsession. Washington backed cruel military dictators throughout Central and South America who employed "death squads" and other repression to thwart socialist uprisings. Thousands of Hispanic labor leaders, university students and other liberals became the "disappeared," covertly abducted and murdered.

After socialist-minded Jacobo Arbenz was elected president of Guatemala in 1951, he confiscated idle land of America's United Fruit Company and gave it to peasants. In Washington, top officials of the Republican Eisenhower administration were Secretary of State John Foster Dulles and his brother, CIA Director Allen Dulles, both large United Fruit shareholders. Eisenhower secretly sent the CIA to arm a rebel army and overthrow Arbenz, installing a military dictator in his place. Arbenz fled into exile and ruin. His daughter committed suicide.

Meanwhile, in the United States, fear of leftist "subversives" flared in the 1950s in the hysterical phenomenon called McCarthyism. It became a witch-hunt aimed mostly at intellectuals, labor leaders, writers, professors, movie performers, musicians and other left-leaning figures -- many of whom had attended communist rallies or leftist book clubs during agonies of the Great Depression. As America suffered in the 1930s, many in the intelligentsia had considered communism as a possible cure, and membership in the American Communist Party rose to 50,000 in 1939.

Joseph McCarthy was a tough-talking, hard-drinking, GOP senator from Wisconsin. He drew little attention until 1950 when he came to my state of West Virginia, addressed the Republican Women's Club of Wheeling, pulled out a sheet of paper and declared that it contained names of 205 secret communists working for the State Department. Later he said his list had fifty-seven names.

The allegation that the government was infiltrated by many unpatriotic "subversives" flared across America. Congress launched more than 100 investigations altogether. Right-wing patriotic committees and state-level "loyalty review boards" sought to ferret out hidden reds. During the 1952 Republican convention, McCarthy said it was crucial to "dislodge the traitors" undermining America. Governments began requiring employees to sign loyalty oaths.

Congressional hearings into subversion became an American inquisition. Before television cameras, McCarthy accused and berated hundreds of witnesses, helped by a surly assistant, Roy Cohn. McCarthy forced the State Department to remove leftist books from overseas libraries, and some of the books were burned. The House Un-American Activities Committee did likewise. Scores of Hollywood figures were called before the committee and denounced. Ten producers, writers and actors refused to answer questions. The "Hollywood Ten" cited the First Amendment's right of speech and assembly as protection against testifying -- but it didn't work, and all ten were sent to prison for contempt. A Hollywood blacklist developed to block suspected reds from working in movies.

Later, many congressional witnesses invoked the Fifth Amendment's protection against self-incrimination, and escaped jailing. However, "taking the Fifth" before a loyalty committee wrecked many careers.

Privately, FBI Director J. Edgar Hoover led a huge purge of government employees suspected of alleged communist sympathies. Thousands were dismissed. Often, neither victims nor their attorneys (if they could find any lawyers willing to defend them) were told the evidence against them, or the names of persons accusing them. Careers were destroyed. The left-leaning National Lawyers Guild was among few groups that would help the accused federal workers. Hoover secretly sent FBI agents fourteen times to burgle the National Lawyers Guild office.

Amid the hysteria over "subversion," security clearance was revoked for J. Robert Oppenheimer, father of the atomic bomb, and great numbers of others suffered ugly consequences. One report says: "The number imprisoned is in the hundreds, and some ten or twelve thousand lost their jobs…. In the film industry, more than three hundred actors, authors and directors were denied work in the United States through the unofficial Hollywood blacklist."

The Reverend Billy James Hargis led a national anti-communist religious movement, also attacking racial integration, sex education, the United Nations and other liberal targets. He claimed that he wrote a speech for Sen. McCarthy. Hargis's career later crashed after it was revealed that he seduced both male and female students at his born-again college in Tulsa.

Gradually, a backlash grew against McCarthy's crusade. Congressman George H. Bender said: "McCarthyism has become a synonym for witch-hunting, Star Chamber methods." Senator Margaret Chase Smith gave a floor speech denouncing "character assassination" and attacks on "the right to hold unpopular beliefs." She decried "cancerous tentacles of know-nothing-suspect-everything attitudes." Other senators joined her. Commentator Elmer Davis said the anti-communist inquisition was a "general attack… on all people who think and write…. In short, on the freedom of the mind."

McCarthy's downfall occurred in 1954 during hearings in which he claimed that secret reds were undermining the Army. He attacked the Army's attorney, Joseph Welch, by saying a young man in Welch's Boston office had belonged to the National Lawyers Guild. On national television, Welch replied:

"Until this moment, senator, I think I never really gauged your cruelty or your recklessness.... Have you no sense of decency, sir, at long last? Have you left no sense of decency."

Destruction followed swiftly. Later in 1954, the Senate voted overwhelmingly to "condemn" McCarthy for his conduct. He was disgraced. He died in 1957, reportedly from conditions worsened by alcoholism.

His right-hand aide, Roy Cohn, eventually faced criminal charges and was disbarred, just before his death in 1986.

In a sense, liberals won the struggle over McCarthyism. They were the chief target of the inquisition, and they gained vindication when the witch-hunt was discredited.

Actually, the 1950s upheaval wasn't America's first "red scare." A similar episode happened a generation earlier, around 1920, just after Russia's Bolshevik Revolution sent panic through capitalist western societies.

In that era, a few bomb-throwing anarchists still caused bloodshed. A Wall Street bomb on Sept. 1, 1920, killed thirty-eight people and wounded 141. An anarchist had shot President William McKinley in 1901.

In 1919, several major strikes were spurred by the leftist International Workers of the World, which roused fears of communism. That same year, small bombs were sent to homes of various American leaders, causing little harm.

Attorney General A. Mitchell Palmer ordered arrest and deportation of six thousand "undesirables," mostly foreign immigrants suspected of communism. The "Palmer raids" were a sensation. He also warned that a left-wing revolution would attempt to seize the government on May Day 1920. When it didn't happen, he was ridiculed, and his plan to run for president fizzled.

In the huge wave of arrests, police found only three guns. Supposed evidence mostly evaporated, and nearly all the suspects were freed. One journalist wrote: "The whole lot were about as dangerous as a flea on an elephant."

The first red scare, like the second, ended not with a bang but a whimper.

The Great Society

Another golden age of liberalism -- rivaling Franklin Roosevelt's "New Deal" of the 1930s -- came in the 1960s when President Lyndon Johnson's "Great Society" scored an amazing array of breakthroughs.

It coincided with the historic counterculture upheaval that spurred America's sexual revolution, women's liberation, "green" environmentalism and other liberal transformations.

First, politics: The 1964 election gave Congress a large Democratic majority, and Democratic President Johnson seized the opportunity to pass landmark social changes.

Four different new laws locked in black equality, guaranteeing African Americans (1) the right to vote, wiping out bigoted southern tests that had blocked blacks from the polls, (2) equality in public accommodations, (3) equality in job opportunity, and (4) equality in housing. These breakthroughs infuriated white southern racists and gradually drove Dixie -- formerly the Democratic "Solid South" -- into the conservative Republican Party.

LBJ, a master manipulator, also gained passage of these monumental advances:

Medicare, providing health treatment to retirees.

Medicaid, giving care to the poor.

The Job Corps to train high-school dropouts for brighter futures.

Headstart to give lower-income tots an early school advantage.

Public radio and television, commercial-free educational broadcasting.

Consumer protection laws, guarding against scams.

Strong laws against industrial air, water and land pollution.

Rent supplements to help less-privileged families have better homes.

Federal aid to public schools, letting the national government set education standards.

Truth-in-lending, to save borrowers from hidden costs.

Truth-in-packaging, to halt misleading product claims.

Immigration reform, erasing national-origin quotas.

The Appalachian Redevelopment Act to create jobs in poor hills.

Volunteers in Service to America (VISTA), a domestic version of the Peace Corps.

Upward Bound and the Neighborhood Youth Corps to boost prospects for low-income teens.

Expansion of the federal food stamp program for poor families.

The school breakfast program.

Senior citizen meal programs.

The National Foundation on the Arts and Humanities.

A National Cultural Center, which became the John F. Kennedy Center for the Performing Arts.

The Hirshhorn Museum and Sculpture Garden added to the Smithsonian Institution.

High-speed trains between Washington and New York.

Meat and poultry safety laws.

Cigarette labels warning of lung cancer and other diseases.

The Endangered Species Act.

The National Trails System Act.

The Solid Waste Disposal Act.

The National Historic Preservation Act.

The Wild and Scenic Rivers Act.

And many, many others.

Altogether, Johnson's White House requested 252 laws, and 226 of them passed. It was a cascade of liberal improvements for America.

Simultaneously, America was transformed by the youth rebellion of the 1960s. Drafting young men to be sent into jungle slaughter in Vietnam sparked ferocious resistance, especially on college campuses. It became a stormy time of draft-card burning, mass rallies, college building seizures and other tumult. National Guard killings of Kent

State University protesters in Ohio intensified emotions.

Birth-control pills liberated young women from constant fear of pregnancy, so the sexual revolution blossomed. Recreational sex and cohabitation without marriage soared. Censorship laws were struck down, so sexuality pervaded movies, magazines, books and entertainment.

Young rebels of the 1960s became more accepting of blacks, gays, Asians, Native Americans and other minorities -- groups formerly excluded from majority white society -- thus a trend toward multiculturalism grew.

Some immature excesses of "sex, drugs and rock-and-roll" marked the era. Conservative older Americans were dismayed. Former liberal Democrat Ronald Reagan, who became the right-wing Republican governor of California, saw pickets carrying signs declaring "Make Love, Not War," and said the young people "didn't look capable of doing either."

Nonetheless, the stormy Sixties, like the Thirties, propelled America leftward in profound ways that never can be undone.

Backlash

Liberal advances can trigger conservative counterattacks. That's what struck my town of Charleston, West Virginia, in 1974. A violent fundamentalist uprising against "godless textbooks" brought bombings, shootings and raging brawls, sending "religious right" preachers to jail and prison.

It happened in a period when religious conservatives were fighting back against the liberal upheaval of the turbulent 1960s. That upheaval included a rise of multiculturalism and inclusion of more minority voices alongside those of the white majority. Eventually, school textbooks were revised to include minority concerns that hadn't received much attention previously. This triggered an Appalachian evangelical backlash.

Rock-throwing mobs forced schools to close. Two schools and the board of education office were bombed. Two people were shot. Coal miners struck to support the religious protest. Ku Klux Klansmen and right-wing kooks flocked to Charleston. Some residents tried to form a separate county. A preacher and his followers discussed murdering families who wouldn't join a school boycott. The minister finally went to prison.

During this nightmare, Charleston acquired a national image somewhat like

Dayton, Tennessee, home of the "Scopes monkey trial," the 1925 clash over evolution.

Ironically, the whole Kanawha County insurrection was pointless, because the schoolbooks were just routine texts. Their sins existed only in the fevered imagination of the zealots.

The uprising began when the Reverend Charles Meadows went before the legislature in 1969 to demand a return of the death penalty. He testified that he would "be glad to pull the switch myself" at executions.

Then he attacked sex education in Kanawha schools. He rented an arena and invited "Bible-believing Christians" to a rally against the "pornography" of sex education. Committees were formed. A movement grew.

Alice Moore, wife of a born-again pastor, became the movement's candidate for the school board in 1970. She said sex education was part of a "humanistic, atheistic attack on God." Church groups poured money into her campaign. She won and became the board's ayatollah, supporting Bibles for students and expulsion of pregnant girls.

Moore's moralizing had minor effect until 1974, when new textbooks were up for adoption. She denounced the books as "godless," citing chapters and passages featuring minority dissidents. A protest grew. Twenty-seven fundamentalist clergymen called the texts "immoral and indecent." (Rascals like me hunted for indecency in the books, but found only ordinary school topics.)

On the night of the adoption vote, a thousand protesters surrounded the board office. Despite this menace, members voted three-to-two for the books. Afterward, a group called Christian American Parents picketed stores owned by approving board members.

When school opened, evangelists urged "true Christians" to keep their children home. Attendance fell twenty percent -- moreso in the poor eastern end of the county. The Rev. Marvin Horan led a rally of two thousand protesters. Mobs surrounded schools and blockaded school bus garages. Teachers were threatened. So were families who didn't join the boycott.

During a school board meeting, several beefy protesters moved to the front of the chamber, surrounded board members, and shouted "Jew-lover, nigger-lover, Hitler-lover." They beat the school superintendent and three board members before order was restored.

About 3,500 coal miners went on strike against the texts, and began picketing Charleston industries. Flying rocks, screams and danger were constant. Frightened people in eastern Kanawha began carrying pistols. Many school buses couldn't run -- and then textbook pickets halted city buses, leaving eleven thousand low-income Kanawha Valley people without transportation.

Pickets surrounded a truck terminal, and a terminal janitor fired a shot which wounded one. Other pickets beat the janitor savagely. The next day, an armed man panicked when pickets surged toward him. He fired a shot that wounded a bystander. Two book protesters were jailed for smashing windshields.

The school board got a court injunction against disrupters, but it didn't help. Finally the superintendent closed schools, saying the safety of children couldn't be guaranteed. Schools also closed in two adjoining counties.

Network television crews swarmed to Charleston. A cameraman was trounced by protesters at a protest rally. The Rev. Ezra Graley led a march on the state Capitol and filed a federal suit against the textbooks. Graley and other ministers were jailed for contempt of the court injunction.

Schools reopened. The boycott resumed. The Rev. Charles Quigley prayed for God to kill board members who endorsed the books. A grade school was hit by a Molotov cocktail. Five shots hit a school bus. A dynamite blast damaged another grade school. A bigger blast damaged the school central office.

Near-riot conditions continued. Robert Dornan of California, a pornography foe, addressed a crowd of three thousand. Dornan was sent by Citizens for Decency Through Law, a national organization led by Charles Keating, who later went to prison for savings-and-loan fraud.

Protesters started born-again schools. A fundamentalist magistrate led an attempt to make eastern Kanawha a separate county.

Minister Horan and three of his followers were indicted for the bombings. Ku Klux Klan leaders led a Charleston rally to support them. An imperial wizard from Georgia said the Kanawha textbooks contained "the most vulgar, vile and filthy words in print" -- which was odd, since non-fundamentalists couldn't find any obscenities in them.

During the trial in 1975, other followers said Horan had led the dynamite plot, telling them there was "a time to kill." They said the plotters talked of wiring dynamite caps into the gas tanks of cars in which families were driving their children to school during the boycott. All four defendants went to federal prison.

Horan's conviction ended the protest. Other leaders lost face. Minister Meadows left his church after admitting involvement with a woman religion teacher. Minister Graley's wife left him and he sued to recover the luxury car she took. School board member Moore abruptly left the state.

Looking back, it was a season of madness -- a frenzy over nothing, like the ferment among believers who thought the moon-and-stars logo on Procter & Gamble soap was a secret sign of Satan. The Kanawha chaos showed how zealots can turn trivia into tragedy. It made the holy wars of India and elsewhere a bit more comprehendible.

It was a sobering example of conservative backlash against liberal progress.

Current times

In a speech to the 1992 Republican convention, presidential aspirant Pat Buchanan famously said: "There is a religious war going on in this country. It is a cultural war, as critical to the kind of nation we shall be as the Cold War itself. For this war is for the soul of America."

Buchanan made it clear that enemies in the war were Democrats who wanted "to go back to the discredited liberalism of the 1960s and the failed liberalism of the 1970s." He said they wanted "unrestricted abortion on demand… homosexual rights, discrimination against religious schools, women in combat units" and "the raw sewage of pornography that so terribly pollutes our popular culture." He said Republicans stand "against the amoral idea that gay and lesbian couples should have the same standing in law as married men and women."

Buchanan was correct: a culture war was raging in 1992, and it still rages today. On one side are the GOP and its Tea Party and gun-zealot militias and the white evangelical "religious right" that wants a return to the prim and prejudiced 1950s. On the other side are liberal progressives and secular humanists who want more equality, more fairness, more human rights and more opportunity for everyone.

Roots of the current confrontation go back more than a half-century. They consist of a string of liberal victories, mostly won in the Supreme Court. When public prejudice prevents elected legislators from acting, appointed-for-life federal judges often enforce the Bill of Rights and protect minorities. The legendary "Warren Court" in the 1950s and 1960s, led by reformer Chief Justice Earl Warren, transformed America, and subsequent courts extended the liberal wave. Examples:

In 1954 (*Brown v. Board of Education*), the Supreme Court wiped out school segregation, a colossal blow against America's entrenched racial divide. The landmark decision caused many white southerners to send their children to white-only private schools, rather than let them mix with dark-skinned children -- but the Democratic Carter administration later revoked tax exemption for such "segregation academies."

In 1962 (*Engel v. Vitale*), the court outlawed teacher-led mandatory prayers in public schools, calling them a clear violation of the separation of church and state. A year later (*Abington School District v. Schempp*), it banned devotional Bible-reading in schools. Fundamentalists across America erupted in rage, and the battle has never stopped since. Representative George Andrews of Alabama protested: "They put the Negroes in the schools, and now they've driven God out."

In 1963 (*Gideon v. Wainwright*), justices decreed that poor defendants are entitled to defense lawyers -- and in 1966 (*Miranda v. Arizona*), they ruled that suspects must be given warnings before they blurt out self-incriminating statements.

In 1964 (*Grove Press Inc. v. Gerstein*), the high court specified that lurid sexual descriptions in Henry Miller's *Tropic of Cancer* aren't obscene. Many similar rulings over the years gradually erased sexual censorship in America.

In 1965 (*Griswold v. Connecticut*), the court ruled that married couples have a right to practice birth control in the privacy of their bedrooms. In 1972 (*Eisenstadt v. Baird*), after Warren had left the bench, justices extended the same right to unmarried couples.

In 1967 (Loving v. Virginia), the high court let mixed-race couples wed. The well-named case lifted a Virginia prison sentence that had been imposed on a white man and his black wife, Richard and Mildred Loving, because they married.

In 1973 (*Roe v. Wade*), justices ruled that American women and girls have a right to terminate pregnancies in early months. This historic decision allowed safe modern clinics and erased the ugly era of back-alley abortions that killed many young women. It also unleashed decades of protest by fundamentalists who think a human soul is created each time an egg is fertilized. "Pro-life" pickets and attacks became common at women's clinics. America even suffered "pro-life murder" as a few extremists killed doctors and nurses.

In 2003 (*Lawrence v. Texas*), the high court struck down final remaining state "sodomy" laws that put gays in prison for homosexual acts.

In 2015 (*Young v. United Parcel Service*), justices guaranteed that women cannot be laid off from their jobs just because they become pregnant, if their employer offers lighter work for other temporarily limited workers.

Time after time, the judiciary branch proved to be the last-trench defender of individual and minority rights, when the legislative branch wouldn't act. The high court delivered liberal victory after victory -- propelling conservatives and fundamentalists into a broad-spectrum counterattack.

Amid this snowballing culture war, evangelist Jerry Falwell teamed up with actress Anita Bryant in 1977 to attack gay equality. In 1979, he created the Moral Majority, a political machine through which born-again people supported conservative politicians. He called for church members to save the nation from "the growing tide of permissiveness and moral decay." Soon, Falwell backed many Republican goals such as tax cuts for the rich, more military spending, and the like.

Other religious-right political groups arose: Focus on the Family, the American Family Association, Concerned Women for America and the Religious Roundtable. The latter was created by evangelist James Robison, who told fifteen thousand cheering believers at a 1980 Texas rally for Republican Ronald Reagan:

"I'm sick and tired of hearing about all of the radicals and the perverts and the liberals and the leftists and the communists coming out of the closet. It's time for God's people to come out of the closet."

Evangelical politics helped sweep Reagan into the White House, but he failed to deliver Puritanical victories preachers had expected. The religious right was scorned by many American thinkers and leaders. Even former Republican presidential nominee Barry Goldwater denounced it as shallow bigotry. In 1989, Falwell abandoned the Moral Majority, and evangelist Pat Robertson launched a similar group, the Christian Coalition -- but it had no better success than the first right-wing church organization.

America was evolving, shifting leftward, despite all the sound and fury from the right. In 1983, racist Republican Senator Jesse Helms of North Carolina waged a sixteen-day filibuster to block a national holiday for black martyr Martin Luther King Jr. -- but he failed.

The election of America's first black president was a pinnacle for liberalism. It repudiated centuries of conservative-supported racial segregation and white superiority claims. It elevated America in the eyes of the world.

President Barack Obama inherited a nightmare when he took office in 2009. Previous conservative "deregulation" had loosened safeguards against securities abuse. As a result, some Wall Street manipulators "bundled" groups of shaky subprime mortgages into securities, induced rating agencies to brand them AAA, and peddled them to millions of investors. When the flimsy mortgages failed, it triggered the Great Recession, the worst economic collapse since the Great Depression. Millions of Americans lost jobs, and huge numbers of mortgages were foreclosed. Hardship was suffered across the country, forcing the new administration into intense rescue efforts.

The new president launched several progressive changes. One of his first acts upon taking office was to strike down a ban on federal funding for stem cell research, which had been imposed by Republican President George W. Bush to please fundamentalists. Stem cells are primitive units that mimic any tissue around them. They promise many medical cures by regrowing healthy tissue to heal diseased hearts, damaged spinal cords, lost brain matter, and so forth. But such research is opposed by evangelicals who think cutting open frozen fertilized eggs to obtain their stem cells kills human souls contained in the eggs. Scientific-minded people dismiss this claim as silly.

New President Obama also struck down past barriers that forbade gays to serve in the military. Under him, Congress passed the Lilly Ledbetter Act helping women sue their employers if they are paid less than male employees for equal work. Various other liberal advances were secured.

Obama's greatest achievement occurred in 2010, when Congress had enough Democratic members to pass his landmark Affordable Care Act. It extended health insurance to millions more Americans by expanding Medicaid coverage to a broader range of lower-income families, and by creating online exchanges through which competing insurers offer policies. Federal subsidies defray part of the cost for most of those policies. At latest count, nearly twenty million Americans have gained coverage from the ACA, saving them from the hazards of lacking health care.

The health reform also requires every medical insurance plan (except those of churches) to provide free birth control to women workers who want it. And it lets young people remain under their parents' coverage until age twenty-six. And it forbids insurers to deny care for people with pre-existing ailments.

Republicans waged a fierce battle to kill "ObamaCare." They voted sixty times in Congress to revoke the ACA. After the Supreme Court allowed states to opt out of the Medicaid expansion, almost two dozen GOP-controlled states did so, denying care to millions of low-income folks -- even though the federal government pays nearly all costs. It was a remarkable display of cruelty.

Some pious employers claimed that their "religious freedom" would be trampled if health plans of their businesses provided free contraceptives to women employees. These conservatives won a marginal Supreme Court victory in 2014 (*Burwell v. Hobby Lobby*) that let a tiny fringe of Puritanical employers elude the contraception mandate. But millions of American women gained better birth control.

Actually, universal health care for everyone should be a human right in America, as it is in most other modern democracies. Eventually, this country should adopt a complete, government-run, "single-payer" system eliminating commercial insurers and suppressing medical costs. That's a crusade for the next generation of liberals.

Political conflict is ferocious in America. Hundreds of millions of dollars are spent on intense campaigns, much of it for slanted, exaggerated, smearing "attack ads." Republicans have gained numerous victories at state and congressional levels.

But the tide of liberalism flows, regardless. In the 2012 election, while President Obama won a second term, voters in three states (Maine, Maryland and Washington) approved same-sex weddings, and two states (Colorado and Washington) approved recreational pot-puffing, and several openly gay candidates were elected.

A *Business Week* column called the 2012 returns a "liberal landslide."

Incidentally, Obama became the first president to publicly acknowledge secular Americans who don't attend church. In his inaugural speech, he declared: "We are a nation of Christians and Muslims, Jews and Hindus -- and non-believers." Later, he cited the same diversity. He broke a barrier in 2010 by inviting the Secular Coalition for America to the White House.

During the Obama administration, a spontaneous protest movement caused camp-ins across America, raising echoes of Coxey's

Army in the 1890s and veteran "bonus marchers" who flocked to Washington in 1932.

It began when a liberal Canadian magazine suggested in 2011 that American progressives should "occupy Wall Street" to denounce the elite one percent of rich financiers who hogged an ever-increasing share of the nation's wealth and exerted excessive control over politicians. So a throng of volunteer protesters began assembling.

First, labor unions sponsored a massive march through Wall Street. Also, a group of artists posed nude until they were arrested. Finally, a large band of campers began sleeping `at Zuccotti Park to show their contempt for the one percent at the top. "We are the ninety-nine percent" became their mantra.

The campers demanded forgiveness of student loans and other steps to reduce America's worsening inequality. Food and money donations supplied the hundreds of protesters. The camp-in proceeded for two months, amid clashes with police and complaints about sanitation.

The movement drew a spotlight to the mammoth gap between rich and poor. Rebel filmmaker Michael Moore backed the campers, pointing out that "the one percent have just one percent of the vote."

President Obama saluted the movement: "I think it expresses the frustrations Americans feel, that we had the biggest financial crisis since the Great Depression, huge collateral damage all through the country."

Police finally cleared out the New York campers -- but similar "occupy" encampments sprang up in many American cities and several university campuses. The movement gradually faded, but it reinforced national awareness of the spreading gulf between the privileged elite and the middle class.

Gay equality

Despite all the stunning breakthroughs of science, researchers still haven't found a cause of homosexuality. Various theories -- that it arises from a weak father and strong mother -- or from variations in the hypothalamus -- or from DNA differences -- remain unverified. The American Psychological Association says:

> "There is no consensus among scientists about the exact reasons that an individual develops a heterosexual, bisexual, gay, or lesbian orientation. Although much research has examined the possible genetic, hormonal, developmental, social, and cultural influences on sexual orientation, no findings have emerged that permit scientists to conclude that sexual orientation is determined by any particular factor or factors. Many think that nature and nurture both play complex roles; most people experience little or no sense of choice about their sexual orientation."

That last line -- "little or no sense of choice" -- is crucial. It means that gays have no control over their orientation, and cannot be blamed for it. Puritanical fundamentalists constantly claim that same-sex inclination is evil, and that gays "choose" it. This claim is absurd. Nobody would choose to be an outcast, despised by mainstream society, taunted and ridiculed, even sometimes attacked physically or murdered.

All that can be said with certainty is that a small percentage of humanity (scientists cannot even find the correct ratio) seem to be born with an orientation different from the majority. The condition is baffling to most "straights." Since they cannot understand it, some heterosexuals feel hostility or revulsion or contempt for gays. But that's shallow. When you don't understand something, it's best to avoid harsh judgment. "Straights" simply should accept gays as part of society, and give them opportunity to fashion the best lives possible for themselves.

When I was a young news reporter in the 1950s -- back when prison terms awaited any gays who were caught -- I secretly interviewed a West Virginia State University professor who privately acknowledged his orientation. He said "the mark of sorrow" was upon him and his clandestine colleagues, and they could do nothing about it. I printed his story, with his identity concealed.

The mark of sorrow has cursed gays since prehistoric time. Not only the Bible but also other moral codes targeted them for death.

In the year 390, early Christian emperor Theodosius I mandated that gay men must be burned alive. After Islam arose, Caliph Al-Hadi decreed death to gays in 786. Through the Middle Ages, various European countries executed gays. Knight Richard von Hohenberg and his squire were burned at the stake as a pair of lovers in 1482 at Zurich. In France, writer Jacques Chausson was burned in 1661 for attempting to seduce the son of a nobleman. England's Buggery Act of 1534 mandated death, and the penalty remained in effect until 1861, with the last execution in 1835.

Gradually, liberal tolerance began to reduce the terrible vengeance inflicted on gays in western civilization -- but much of the Islamic world and Africa haven't relented. During the 1970s, many American states quietly replaced their old "sodomy" laws with 'sex offender" statutes, and gay sex no longer was a crime. However, a few conservative states still prosecuted "sodomites." That ended in 2003 when the Supreme Court ruled in *Lawrence v. Texas* that lovemaking between consenting adult same-sex pairs wasn't illegal.

However, seventy-five nations around the world still criminalize gay sex, and ten mandate death. Reports said Iran executed more than four thousand for homosexuality after the Ayatollah Khomeini created a cruel theocracy in 1979. *The Washington Post* recently listed these other nine Islamic or half-Islamic countries that kill gays, mostly under Sharia law: Iraq, Mauritania, Nigeria, Qatar, Saudi Arabia, Somalia, Sudan, United Arab Emirates and Yemen.

In America, amazingly rapid acceptance of gays snowballed in the 21st century. At first, a few states legalized "civil unions" giving homosexual pairs some legal protections of marriage. Then a crusade for complete gay wedlock stampeded. A few states and federal court rulings authorized it. Young Americans generally accepted the notion.

Fundamentalists, Catholics and conservatives howled in protest. Republican presidential candidate and evangelist Mike Huckabee declared in a West Virginia speech that allowing gays to marry would lead to wedlock between people and animals.

After hesitating, President Obama endorsed gay marriage. In mid-2015, the Supreme Court ruled in *Obergefell v. Hodges* that gays are entitled to marry, just as heterosexuals are. Five liberal justices concluded that equal treatment is required by the large motto over the Supreme Court building in Washington: "Equal Justice Under Law." Four conservative justices protested, but they lost.

It was another major liberal victory in the never-ending progressive struggle for equality and compassion.

Scholars watch the tides

In 2004, former U.S. Labor Secretary Robert Reich wrote a book subtitled *Why Liberals Will Win the Battle for America*. He argued that the populace is more compassionate than the tone set by conservatives who dominate government. He said most Americans have "a bedrock sense of public, or common, morality" which sympathizes with ordinary folks, not the privileged elite favored by conservatives.

"Republicans have posed the deepest moral question of any society: whether we're in it together," Reich wrote. "Their answer is we're not." But Reich said conscientious people "should proclaim, loudly and clearly, we are."

In his book, the ex-labor secretary outlined:

"The classical liberal ideas that emerged in the seventeenth and eighteenth centuries and took root in America soil sought -- for the first time in human history -- to improve the wellbeing of all people, not just the rich and the privileged. Liberalism has stood for an economic system that betters the lives of average working people, and for a democracy that gives voice to the little guy. That liberal tradition animated American abolitionists of the nineteenth century who fought against slavery. It inspired suffragettes who demanded that women have the right to vote. And it motivated civil rights workers who put their lives on the line for equal rights.

"American liberalism... moved reformers at the turn of the last century to stand firm against monopolies and political corruption. It inspired progressives to battle for safety, health, and food and drug regulations. In the wake of the Great Crash of 1929, it led New Dealers to regulate banking and clean up Wall Street. As the Depression deepened, it prompted them to create Social Security, unemployment insurance and a minimum wage.... The same liberal spirit aroused labor leaders to fight for better pay and working conditions for average working people. And it animated public-works spending to put millions of Americans back to work....

"Liberals have always stood in sharp opposition to fanaticism and violence, and against religious bigotry, totalitarianism, and nationalist zealotry.... They've held to the goal of an international community. After World War II, they created the United Nations and international economic institutions....

"These ideals -- this profound insistence that Americans are all in it together, this search for practical reforms to make democracy and the economy work better for average people, this bulwark against bigotry and fanaticism, this smart internationalism, this demand for decency and tolerance -- this is the true, robust liberalism."

Reich pointed out that, "before the New Deal, liberalism was mostly about protecting people's freedom," but, ever since the Depression, progressives have championed a public safety net to protect average families from calamity.

In 2016, Boston University religion professor Stephen Prothero wrote *Why Liberals Win the Culture Wars (Even When They Lose Elections).* He says conservatives often feel society around them shifting away from their cherished privileges and prejudices -- for example, they feel "anxiety about the demise of the patriarchal family or Anglo-American dominance or 'Christian America.'" Too late, they raise an outcry and fight a furious resistance, but the trend can't be stopped.

"In almost every case since the founding of the republic," he wrote, "conservatives have fired the first shots in our culture wars. Equally often, liberals have won.... A liberal win becomes part of the new status quo and eventually fades from our collective memory. No conservative today wants to disenfranchise Mormons or outlaw five o'clock cocktails. So these victories no longer even appear to be 'liberal.' They are simply part of what it means to be an American."

The professor added:

"America's culture wars are won by liberals.... Gays and lesbians get marriage. An 'infidel' (Jefferson) and then a 'papist' (Kennedy) get the White House. Nearly as predictably as night follows day, those who declare war on 'infidels' or Catholics or the sins of the 1920s or the abominations of the 1960s go down in defeat. Liberals win because they typically have the force of American traditions on their side, not least the force of the Bill of Rights itself, which on any fair reading protects the rights of minorities against the impositions of majorities. Liberals also win because the causes conservatives pick to rev up their supporters are, surprisingly, lost from the start."

Dr. Prothero spotlights five religious-racial-moral battles in America. The first was a bitter showdown in the 1790s when conservative churchmen branded Thomas Jefferson a "howling atheist" in league with violent radicals of the French Revolution. The struggle involved dispute over whether America was "a Christian nation."

Elections of 1796 and 1800 "turned into a cosmic battle between God and the devil, and America's first culture war was on," Prothero wrote. Alexander Hamilton called Jefferson "an atheist in religion and a fanatic in politics." Amid the tumult, "conservatives scapegoated immigrants as 'hordes of ruffians' and 'revolutionary vermin'" (somewhat like today's Republican denunciations of Hispanics and Muslims).

In the end, Jefferson triumphed, and America became more inclusive of dissimilar people.

The second culture war cited by the professor was a wave of violent "nativist" Protestant attacks on Catholics around America. In 1844, Catholic-Protestant hatreds triggered a cannon battle in the streets of Philadelphia, killing dozens. Anti-Catholic riots and church-burning ensued into the 1850s, spawning the "America for Americans" Know-Nothing Party, which won 75 seats in Congress in 1854. Gradually, hatred of Catholics receded, but Protestant prejudice lingered until John F. Kennedy won the presidency in 1960.

The third culture war was hostility and violence toward Mormons and their polygamy practice. Latter-Day Saints founder Joseph Smith and his brother were murdered by an anti-Mormon mob in Illinois in 1844. Also, "Mormon leaders would be sued, jailed, beaten, stripped naked, tarred and feathered, and murdered," the professor wrote. But this wave eventually faded, like bigotry against Catholics.

The fourth cited culture war was Prohibition in the 1920s, after evangelists and fundamentalists succeeded in banning alcohol. The struggle included alarms over flappers, jazz, race-mixing, smoking, cosmetics, hair-bobbing, Sunday golf -- and even evolution, as crystallized by the "Scopes Monkey Trial" in Tennessee in 1925. Government-enforced sobriety bred bootleggers, organized crime, and bribery of police and prosecutors. In the end, liberals won the right for Americans to drink if they wished. Conservative churches were defeated, and Prohibition ended.

The final and current culture war rose as a backlash against the tumultuous 1960s, when young Americans loosed the sexual revolution and war-denouncing counterculture. Racial desegregation, women's right to choose abortion, and banning of government-led school prayer further outraged right-wingers. Conservatives "saw American society drifting away from them, erasing forms of culture they held dear," Prothero says.

As a counterattack, the "religious right" Moral Majority rose, and white evangelicals put conservative Ronald Reagan in the White House. White-only "segregation academies" were started so conservative families could avoid mixed-race schools. "Family values" became a slogan for hating gays. Pro-life murder occurred when a few zealots killed doctors and nurses at abortion clinics. Claims flared that America is an exceptional "Christian nation."

But slowly, step by step, liberals carried the day. Gays won a nationwide right to marry. President Obama's health care expansion made medicine available to millions of families. Etc.

"Conservatives lost the contemporary culture wars and they lost them badly," professor Prothero says. "As the counterculture mainstreamed, American society continued to drift left." He cites numerous showdowns in which modern conservatives went down to defeat, "the lost causes of conservatism."

"The rage on the right that descended over the United States upon Barack Obama's 2009 inauguration" probably will burn itself out. "Fox News is rapidly being reduced to a rickety shrine to white male identity politics." Young Americans strongly favor marijuana legalization and same-sex marriage. "American culture is much less conservative now than it was in 1999."

Most Americans have accepted liberal victories, but Tea Party hard-liners still sound right-wing trumpets. Will culture wars continue forever? Will progressives keep pushing for more personal freedoms? Dr. Prothero concludes:

"Liberals can take comfort in the fact that they almost always win our cultural battles -- that the arc of American cultural politics bends toward more liberty, not less."

Unstoppable

Demographics suggest a bright future for liberalism in America. Several trends swing left.

The heart of conservatism is white, older, male, less-educated, socially narrow churchgoers, many of them rural. White evangelicals vote Republican by a three-to-one margin. But this cohort keeps shrinking in the United States.

In contrast, rising Hispanics, Asians, blacks, single women, well-educated urbanites and secular young people generally share tolerant views and vote Democratic. They're more welcoming to outsiders like gays, more sympathetic to left-out people. They're expected to dominate the future.

The Census Bureau projects that, sometime around 2040, traditional European whites will slip below half of America's population -- thus every ethnic group will be a minority. Already, the number of minority babies born in America exceeds white infants. The cornerstone of the GOP base, white males, will slip to minor status in coming decades.

Meanwhile, hidebound religion that fuels the Republican Party is fading relentlessly in America and the West. Secular young urban people who say their religion is "none" are soaring, and they generally hold humane liberal views. They have become the largest single bloc in the base of America's Democratic Party.

Of course, not all religious people are conservatives. Black Protestants, Jews, Unitarians, high-steeple mainliners like Episcopalians and even many Catholics (especially Hispanics) generally lean left. But they lack the unified identity of multitudinous white evangelicals. As the churchless grow and evangelicals shrink, liberal values seem destined to become locked tighter into America's mainstream.

The collapse of supernatural religion is a stunning sociological development. After World War II, churchgoing took a nosedive in Europe, Canada, Australia, Japan, New Zealand and other democratic Western regions. Churchy America seemed an exception, but now it is following the secular stampede. All polls since the 1990s find a rapid decrease in worship. The number who list their faith as "none" or "don't know" has passed 50 million adults, constantly climbing. Sociologist Ruy Teixeira wrote about the United States:

"In 1944, eighty percent of adults were white Christians. But things have changed a lot since then. Today, only about fifty-two percent of adults are white Christians. By 2024, that figure will be down to forty-five percent. That means that by the election of 2016, the United States will have ceased to be a white Christian nation. Looking even farther down the road, by 2040 white Christians will be only around thirty-five percent of the population and conservative white Christians, who have been such a critical part of the GOP base, only about a third of that -- a minority within a minority."

London's *Guardian* reported:

"So-called millennials (Americans born between 1982 and 2000) are far more diverse, educated and tolerant than their predecessors. They're also the least-religious generation in America's history -- they're even getting less religious as they age, which is unprecedented -- and the majority of them identify Christianity with harsh political conservatism."

U.S. News & World Report said:

"The fastest-growing religious group in the United States is those with no religious affiliation, and members of that group are leaning dramatically in the Democratic direction.... Three in four of them voted for Barack Obama in the last election.... Secular voters will become an increasingly important component of the Democratic base."

In late 2015, a conservative group, Americans for Limited Government, warned that Republicans are "dying off" in the United States. It said 62 million Americans voted for George W. Bush for president in 2004, but election totals "have been down ever since."

"Republicans have proven unable to expand their voting coalition," the organization lamented. The reason "is simply because there are fewer Republicans who are still alive."

Generations just after World War II were split about 50-50 in their allegiance to the two major political parties, but those aging generations are dwindling. ALG continued:

"Their replacements in the voting-age population at the younger end of the spectrum have unquestioningly skewed Democratic.

Millennials, those born between 1980 and 1996, register 53 percent Democrat or lean-Democrat, compared to 35 percent who are Republican or lean-Republican.... Meaning, quite literally, that the Republican Party is dying off."

Writing in *USA Today*, Rutgers University political scientist Ross Baker said demographic trends seem to show "groups likely to vote for the GOP in steep decline and Democratic-oriented voters surging." He said America may experience "a doubling of new racial minorities -- Hispanics, Asians and multiracial Americans -- coupled with the tepid growth of the nation's aging white population." He said left-leaning analysts hope for "a triumphal procession of likely Democrats -- young and minority voters -- marching boldly along a road to the future lined with the graves of dead Republicans."

However, Dr. Baker warned that "populations do not equal voters.... The very groups predicted to swell the numbers of Democrats are also those least likely to show up at the polls."

Here's an example of rapid social evolution:

As recently as the 1990s, large segments of Americans supported the death penalty. Back then, nearly 80 percent approved of executing those convicted of committing cruel murders. America's pro-death ratio was higher than in other modern democracies. Maybe it was a remnant from harsh Puritan founders who hanged Quakers and "witches." Maybe it was tinged with racism, since few whites are put to death.

Republicans, especially, have always been pro-death, with 87 percent in a 1996 poll wanting executions -- while Democrats and independents were less eager.

However, the public mood changed dramatically. Support for executions dropped greatly, according to a 2015 survey by Pew Research Center. It found that 77 percent of Republicans still want state killings, but only 40 percent of Democrats do -- and a mere 29 percent of Democrats who call themselves liberal. Meanwhile, 57 percent of independents are pro-death.

Think of that: Republicans are almost twice as eager to put people to death as Democrats are.

Pew found that men want executions more (64 percent) than women (49 percent) -- whites back death more (63 percent) than blacks (34 percent) -- and Protestants support death more (63 percent) than Catholics (53 percent) and churchless seculars (48 percent).

By a slight margin, America at large still supports death, but the ratio is approaching 50-50.

Actually, executions are disappearing in America. Since 2004, seven more states have dropped the practice, bringing non-killing states to nineteen. Many others simply don't use the death penalty. Just three states -- Texas, Georgia and Missouri -- perform most executions. Liberal objections to execution slowly are prevailing.

A 2016 Supreme Court case from Pennsylvania alleged that executions are "cruel and unusual punishment," which is banned by the Eighth Amendment in the Bill of Rights. This case offered hope that the death penalty could be wiped out forever. However, the high court refused to hear the case.

Putting people to death is a barbaric leftover from brutal medieval times. Almost every advanced society around the globe halted executions -- except America. I'm proud that my Democrat-led state of West Virginia abandoned the death penalty a half-century ago. I agree with Justice Anthony Kennedy, who wrote in a 2008 case:

"When the law punishes by death, it risks its own sudden descent into brutality, transgressing the constitutional commitment to decency and restraint."

In other words, when society kills people for killing, it sinks to the level of the killers, instead of standing for humane values.

Here's another example of liberal advance:

Nearly everyone knows that Fox News -- owned by right-wing billionaire Rupert Murdoch -- isn't a normal news channel, but is a conservative political outlet. Its commentators present a never-ending flow of far-right rhetoric. The network's claim to be "fair and balanced" is almost a joke.

Some observers predict that Fox slowly will lose its dominance over cable news, because its white viewers are aging and dying, while rising young multicultural Americans hold more tolerant, liberal beliefs. Frank Rich wrote in a *New York* magazine analysis: "Fox

News is a right-wing propaganda machine and at times a racist enterprise."

He acknowledged that Fox is a giant of cable broadcasting -- as large as CNN and MSNBC combined -- but he stressed that cable news is a small fringe of America. Only about 1 million people watch Fox daily. "More people own ferrets than watch Fox News," columnist David Brooks commented.

Fox's viewer group is "more than happy to be cocooned in an echo chamber where its own hopes and fears will be reinforced by other older white 'people like us.'" Rich wrote. "Fox is in essence a retirement community." He continued:

"The network's chauvinistic Christianity... is hardly an inducement to a younger America that is eschewing religious affiliation in numbers larger than any in the history of Pew polling. Fox News's unreconstructed knee-jerk homophobia, most recently dramatized by its almost unanimous defense of the Duck Dynasty patriarch Phil Robertson's likening of gay sex to bestiality, drives away viewers of all ages, but especially the young."

Younger Americans tend to ignore cable news and get most of their information on the Internet.

Rich said the hard-core right will lose steam "once its unifying bete noire [black beast], literal and figurative, Obama, is gone from the White House."

TV host Jerry Springer commented that Rich is correct because "liberals always win." He said it's "the way that humanity progresses…. Ultimately, the conservatives will lose."

One topic that seems to defy liberal reform is the worsening gulf between the ultra-rich and everyone else.

In early 2016, Oxfam International, a worldwide federation of seventeen poverty-fighting agencies, released a report that boggles the mind: A mere sixty-two billionaires now own as much wealth as 3.5 billion people in the bottom half of the world's population. It was a stunning illustration of inequality.

Just five years earlier, it took 388 billionaires to equal the assets of the lower 3.5 billion, but that number was cut by five-sixths. Concentration of riches at the extreme top snowballed rapidly.

Political scientist Jeffrey Winters of Northwestern University said "unprecedented levels of stratification" have reached the highest peak "in all of human history." Regarding the intertwined global economy, he said: "No other system has concentrated wealth as much as this system has."

Part of the widening gulf between the super-rich and the rest is caused by offshore tax havens that let fat-cats hide their money from tax collectors. Raymond Offenheiser, president of Oxfam America, commented:

"Tax havens are at the core of a global system that allows large corporations and wealthy individuals to avoid paying their fair share, depriving governments, rich and poor, of resources they need to provide vital public services and tackle rising inequality."

Giant banks and crafty tax lawyers help the elite conceal their assets, Oxfam said.

Meanwhile, a Dutch research group said the ultra-rich are divided into two groups: self-oriented and social-oriented. The latter segment includes billionaires like Bill Gates, Warren Buffet, Mark Zuckerberg, Richard Branson and others who use their wealth to help humanity. In contrast, the self-oriented mostly hoard for their own families.

Professor Winters said billionaires use their political power to gain government policies that further enrich themselves. He concludes that Americans should "adopt policies that make it harder for the ultra-wealthy to shape our government and our society."

Curbing the terrible gap between the privileged and the public may become one of the next major battlefronts between liberals and conservatives.

Generally, demographic forecasts paint a rosy future for liberalism -- but there's the glitch noted by professor Baker: Secular young independents often ignore politics and don't vote. Maybe they're disgusted by shallow pandering and crudity in campaigns. However, their growing number raises hope that America's public policies will shift. It would be absurd if America becomes a nation with a liberal majority ruled by conservative politicians who win elections.

On rare occasions, there are exceptions to the pattern of liberals trying to expand the public safety net and conservatives trying to curtail it. One happened in 2003 when Republican President George W. Bush added prescription coverage to Medicare for seniors.

Liberalism is driven by a spirit of shared humanity. Virachand Gandhi, an Indian reformer in the 1800s, summed up: "To the liberal-minded, the whole world is a family."

The struggle between right and left is never-ending, erupting in many forms. It has flared and flailed erratically ever since The Enlightenment. Presumably, it will continue forever as issues and disputes evolve.

Phases of the battle may be long and painful, but it's heartening that liberals generally win in the end. Civilization keeps advancing progressively toward compassion and tolerance.

Conservatives mocked their opponents so intensely that "liberal" became a term of scorn in much of America. But quietly, almost glacially, progressive values prevail, because they fit the sense of fairness and decency within the human soul.

As comedienne Janeane Garofalo said: "We can no longer tolerate anti-intellectualism. We can no longer tolerate liberal-bashing, and we can no longer tolerate the politics of the dumb and the mean."

The left is right. Liberals always win.

Insights

"If your workplace is safe; if your children go to school rather than being forced into labor; if you are paid a living wage, including overtime; if you enjoy a 40-hour week and you are allowed to join a union to protect your rights -- you can thank liberals. If your food is not poisoned and your water is drinkable -- you can thank liberals. If your parents are eligible for Medicare and Social Security, so they can grow old in dignity without bankrupting your family -- you can thank liberals. If our rivers are getting cleaner and our air isn't black with pollution; if our wilderness is protected and our countryside is still green -- you can thank liberals. If people of all races can share the same public facilities; if everyone has the right to vote; if couples fall in love and marry regardless of race; if we have finally begun to transcend a segregated society -- you can thank liberals. Progressive innovations like those and so many others were achieved by long, difficult struggles against entrenched power. What defined conservatism, and conservatives, was their opposition to every one of those advances. The country we know and love today was built by those victories for liberalism, with the support of the American people." -- journalist Joe Conason

-----

"Being a liberal is the best thing on earth you can be. You are welcoming to everyone when you're a liberal. You do not have a small mind... I'm total, total, total liberal and proud of it. I'm a total Democrat. I'm anti-Republican. And it's only fair that you know it. I'm liberal -- the 'L' word!" -- actress Lauren Bacall (1924-2014)

"A liberal is a man or woman or a child who looks forward to a better day, a more tranquil night, and a bright, infinite future." -- conductor-composer Leonard Bernstein (1918-1990)

"Without liberals we wouldn't have unions. We wouldn't have environmental protections. We wouldn't have seat belts or birth control or the ACLU! Any of those things!" -- Janeane Garofalo, actress, comedienne and political activist.

"Trying to get today's Republican to accept basic facts is like trying to get your dog to take a pill. You have to feed them the truth wrapped in a piece of boloney, hold their snout shut, and stroke their throats. And even then, just when you think they've swallowed it, they spit it out on the linoleum." -- comedian-iconoclast Bill Maher

-----

"If racism is not the whole of the Tea Party, it is in its heart, along with blind hatred, a total disinterest in the welfare of others, and a full-flowered self-rationalizing refusal to accept the outcomes of elections, or the reality of democracy, or the narrowness of their minds and the equal narrowness of their public support." -- left-wing commentator Keith Olbermann

-----

"The liberals were liberators -- they fought slavery, fought for women to have the right to vote, fought against Hitler, fought to end segregation, fought to end apartheid. Liberals put an end to child labor and they gave us the five-day work week!" -- singer Barbra Streisand

-----

"A liberal man is too broad-minded to take his own side in a quarrel." -- poet Robert Frost (1874-1963)

"The liberal holds that he is true to the republic when he is true to himself. (It may not be as cozy an attitude as it sounds.) He greets with enthusiasm the fact of the journey, as a dog greets a man's invitation to take a walk. And he acts in the dog's way too, swinging wide, racing ahead, doubling back, covering many miles of territory that the man never traverses, all in the spirit of inquiry and the zest for truth. He leaves a crazy trail, but he ranges far beyond the genteel old party he walks with and he is usually in a better position to discover a skunk." -- writer E. B. White (1899-1985)

"The essence of the liberal outlook lies not in what opinions are held, but in how they are held: instead of being held dogmatically, they are held tentatively, and with a consciousness that new evidence may at any moment lead to their abandonment." -- philosopher-mathematician Bertrand Russell (1872-1970)

"A liberal is a man who is right most of the time, but he's right too soon." -- Gregory Nunn

-----

"Liberalism -- it is well to recall this today -- is the supreme form of generosity; it is the right which the majority concedes to minorities and hence it is the noblest cry that has ever resounded in this planet. It announces the determination to share existence with the enemy; more than that, with an enemy which is weak." -- Spanish philosopher José Ortega y Gasset (1883-1955)

"We who are liberal and progressive know that the poor are our equals in every sense except that of being equal to us." -- author-teacher Lionel Trilling (1905-1975)

"People often say with pride, 'I'm not interested in politics.' They might as well say, 'I'm not interested in my standard of living, my health, my job, my rights, my freedoms, my future, or any future.'" -- novelist-journalist Martha Gellhorn (1908-1998), third wife of Ernest Hemingway

-----

"Stay bored and government becomes more of an instrument of the rich and powerful against the rest of America. Get active with your fellow citizens and you might just see more government of, by, and for the people." -- reformer Ralph Nader.

"I believe in a relatively equal society, supported by institutions that limit extremes of wealth and poverty. I believe in democracy, civil liberties and the rule of law. That makes me a liberal, and I'm proud of it." -- Nobel Prize-winning economist Paul Krugman

-----

"I think being a liberal, in the true sense, is being nondoctrinaire, nondogmatic, non-committed to a cause - but examining each case on its merits. Being left of center is another thing; it's a political position. I think most newspapermen by definition have to be liberal; if they're not liberal, by my definition of it, then they can hardly be good newspapermen. If they're preordained dogmatists for a cause, then they can't be very good journalists." -- TV news anchor Walter Cronkite (1916-2009), interview for *Playboy*, 1973

"The liberal soul shall be made fat : and he that watereth shall be watered also himself." -- Proverbs 11:25

"So much of liberalism in its classical sense is taken for granted in the west today and even disrespected. We take freedom for granted, and because of this we don't understand how incredibly vulnerable it is." --

Scottish historian and Harvard professor Niall Ferguson

"Does the mainstream media have a liberal bias? On a couple of things, maybe. Compared to the American public at large, probably a slightly higher percentage of journalists, because of their enhanced power of discernment, realize they know a gay person or two, and are, therefore, less frightened of them." -- comedian-senator Al Franken

-----

"Ultimately, totalitarianism is the only sort of politics that can truly serve the sky-god's purpose. Any movement of a liberal nature endangers his authority and that of his delegates on earth. One God, one King, one Pope, one master in the factory, one father-leader in the family at home." -- iconoclast writer Gore Vidal (1925-2012)

"If capitalism is fair, then unionism must be. If men have a right to capitalize their ideas and the resources of their country, then that implies the right of men to capitalize their labor." -- architect Frank Lloyd Wright (1867-1959)

"The most effective way to restrict democracy is to transfer decision-making from the public arena to unaccountable institutions: kings and princes, priestly castes, military juntas, party dictatorships, or modern corporations." -- reformer Noam Chomsky

-----

"Take sides. Neutrality helps the oppressor, never the victim. Silence encourages the tormentor, never the tormented." -- Nobel Peace Prize winner Elie Wiesel, a Nazi death camp survivor

-----

"The country is governed for the richest, for the corporations, the bankers, the land speculators, and for the exploiters of labor. The majority of mankind are working people. So long as their fair demands - the ownership and control of their livelihoods - are set at naught, we can have neither men's rights nor women's rights. The majority of mankind is ground down by industrial oppression in order that the small remnant may live in ease." -- blind, deaf thinker Helen Keller (1880-1968)

"Justice is the first virtue of social institutions.... Therefore in a just society the liberties of equal citizenship are taken as settled; the rights secured by justice are not subject to political bargaining or to the calculus of social interests." -- philosopher John Rawls (1921-2002), *A Theory of Justice*

"No school can supply an anti-liberal education, or a fascist education, as these terms are contradictory. Liberalism and education are one." -- journalist George Seldes (1890-1995)

"Those who are in a position of strength have a responsibility to protect the weak." -- Thomas Cushman, *A Matter of Principle*

"If you can't afford the good food or if you can't afford health care or if you don't have a job or if your car is dangerous because you can't get it fixed and you DIE, you just lost the game -- bzzzzz -- thanks for playing Extreme Capitalism." -- comic Marc Maron, *Attempting Normal*

"Democracy is... a dynamic way of life that encourages efforts to make society and government always better. The democrat believes that human nature is improved as man's environment is perfected.... The democrat recognizes all the world's people as his brothers, equally good and equally deserving.... The democrat believes in international cooperation and a peaceful world." -- West Virginia State University Dean Edwin Hoffman, *Pathways to Freedom*, 1964

"It rests with the liberals and the tolerant to preserve our civilization. Everything of importance in this world has been accomplished by the free inquiring spirit." -- United Mine Workers President John L. Lewis (1880-1969)

NINETEENTH CENTURY

"I sit on a man's back, choking him and making him carry me, and yet assure myself and others that I am very sorry for him and wish to ease his lot by all possible means -- except by getting off his back. " -- Russian novelist-aristocrat-humanitarian Leo Tolstoy (1828-1910)

"I did not mean that conservatives are generally stupid; I meant that stupid persons are generally conservative. I believe that to be so obvious and undeniable a fact that I hardly think any honorable gentleman will question it." -- thinker John Stuart Mill (1806-1873) during a Parliament debate with Conservative member John Pakington, May 31, 1866

"It still remains unrecognised, that to bring a child into existence without a fair prospect of being able, not only to provide food for its body, but instruction and training for its mind, is a moral crime, both against the unfortunate offspring and against society; and that if the parent does not fulfill this obligation, the state ought to see it fulfilled, at the charge, as far as possible, of the parent." -- John Stuart Mill, *On Liberty*

"Conservatism is the blind and fear-filled worship of dead radicals." -- humorist Mark Twain (1835-1910)

PRESIDENTS, ETC.

"As mankind becomes more liberal, they will be more apt to allow that all those who conduct themselves as worthy members of the community are equally entitled to the protections of civil government. I hope ever to see America among the foremost nations of justice and liberality." -- President George Washington (1732-1799), letter to Roman Catholics, May 15, 1790

"The tax which will be paid for the purpose of education is not more than the thousandth part of what will be paid to kings, priests and nobles who will rise up among us if we leave the people in ignorance." -- President Thomas Jefferson (1743-1826)

"I know of no safe repository of the ultimate power of society but people. And if we think them not enlightened enough, the remedy is not to take the power from them, but to inform them by education." -- Thomas Jefferson

-----

"To impose taxes when the public exigencies require them is an obligation of the most sacred character, especially with a free people." -- President James Monroe (1758-1831)

"The means of defense against foreign danger have been always the instruments of tyranny at home. Among the Romans it was a standing maxim to excite a war, whenever a revolt was apprehended. Throughout all Europe, the armies kept up under the pretext of defending, have enslaved the people." -- President James Madison (1751-1836), *Notes of Debates in the Federal Convention of 1787*

"Labor is prior to, and independent of, capital. Capital is only the fruit of labor, and could never have existed if labor had not first existed. Labor is the superior of capital, and deserves much the higher consideration." -- President Abraham Lincoln (1809-1865), first annual message to Congress, December 3, 1861

"We all agree that neither the government nor political parties ought to interfere with religious sects. It is equally true that religious sects ought not to interfere with the government or with political parties. We believe that the cause of good government and the cause of religion suffer by all such interference." -- President Rutherford B. Hayes (1822-1893)

"The divorce between Church and State ought to be absolute. It ought to be so absolute that no church property anywhere, in any state or in the nation, should be exempt from equal taxation; for if you exempt the property of any church organization, to that extent you impose a tax upon the whole community." -- President James A. Garfield (1831-1881)

"The laboring classes constitute the main part of our population. They should be protected in their efforts peaceably to assert their rights when endangered by aggregated capital, and all statutes on this subject should recognize the care of the state for honest toil, and be framed with a view of improving the condition of the workingman." -- President Grover Cleveland (1837-1908)

"America was established not to create wealth but to realize a vision, to realize an ideal - to discover and maintain liberty among men." -- President Woodrow Wilson (1856-1924)

"I like to pay taxes. With them, I buy civilization." -- Supreme Court Justice Oliver Wendell Holmes Jr. (1841-1935)

"We may have democracy, or we may have wealth concentrated in the hands of a few, but we cannot have both." -- Supreme Court Justice Louis Brandeis (1856-1941)

"Republicans approve of the American farmer -- but they are willing to help him go broke. They stand foursquare for the American home -- but not for housing. They are strong for labor -- but they are stronger for restricting labor's rights. They favor minimum wage -- the smaller the minimum wage the better. They endorse educational opportunity for all -- but they won't spend money for teachers or for schools. They think modern medical care and hospitals are fine -- for people who can afford them. They consider electrical power a great blessing -- but only when the private power companies get their rake-off. They think American standard of living is a fine thing -- so long as it doesn't spread to all the people. And they admire the government of the United

States so much that they would like to buy it." -- President Harry Truman (1884-1972)

"You know that being an American is more than a matter of where your parents came from. It is a belief that all men are created free and equal and that everyone deserves an even break." -- Harry Truman

-----

"Only a fool would try to deprive working men and working women of their right to join the union of their choice." -- President Dwight Eisenhower (1890-1969)

"Should any political party attempt to abolish Social Security, unemployment insurance, and eliminate labor laws and farm programs, you would not hear of that party again in our political history. There is a tiny splinter group, of course, that believes that you can do these things. Among them are a few Texas oil millionaires, and an occasional politician or businessman from other areas. Their number is negligible and they are stupid." -- Dwight Eisenhower, from a private letter

-----

"We will bankrupt ourselves in the vain search for absolute security." -- Dwight Eisenhower

-----

"If a free society cannot help the many who are poor, it cannot save the few who are rich." -- President John F. Kennedy (1917-1963)

"Tolerance implies no lack of commitment to one's own beliefs. Rather it condemns the oppression or persecution of others." -- John F. Kennedy

-----

"Change is the law of life. And those who look only to the past or present are certain to miss the future." -- John F. Kennedy

-----

"Few nations do more than the United States to assist their least-fortunate citizens -- to make certain that no child, no elderly or handicapped citizen, no family in any circumstances in any state, is left without the essential needs for a decent and healthy existence. In too few nations, I might add, are the people aware of the progressive strides this country has taken in demonstrating the humanitarian side of freedom. Our record is a proud one -- and it sharply refutes those who accuse us of thinking only in the materialistic terms of cash registers and calculating machines." -- John F. Kennedy

-----

"Let us think of education as the means of developing our greatest abilities, because in each of us there is a private hope and dream which, fulfilled, can be translated into benefit for everyone and greater strength for our nation." -- John F. Kennedy

-----

"I believe that, as long as there is plenty, poverty is evil." -- Attorney General Robert Kennedy (1925-1968)

"Ultimately, America's answer to the intolerant man is diversity, the very diversity which our heritage of religious freedom has inspired." -- Robert Kennedy

-----

"For all my years in public life, I have believed that America must sail toward the shores of liberty and justice for all. There is no end to that journey, only the next great voyage. We know the future will outlast all of us, but I believe that all of us will live on in the future we make." -- Sen. Edward Kennedy (1932-2009)

"Liberalism, above all, means emancipation -- emancipation from one's fears, his inadequacies, from prejudice, from discrimination... from poverty." -- Vice President Hubert Humphrey (1911-1978)

"It was once said that the moral test of government is how that government treats those who are in the dawn of life, the children; those who are in the twilight of life, the elderly; and those who are in the shadows of life, the sick, the needy and the handicapped." -- Hubert Humphrey

-----

"Compassion is not weakness, and concern for the unfortunate is not socialism." -- Hubert Humphrey

-----

"Today's so-called 'conservatives' don't even know what the word means. They think I've turned liberal because I believe a woman has a right to an abortion. That's a decision that's up to the pregnant woman, not up to the pope or some do-gooders or the Religious Right. It's not a conservative issue at all." -- Republican presidential candidate Barry Goldwater (1909-1998)

"While I am a great believer in the free enterprise system and all that it entails, I am an even stronger believer in the right of our people to live in a clean and pollution-free environment." -- Barry Goldwater

-----

"Mark my word, if and when these preachers get control of the [Republican] party, and they're sure trying to do so, it's going to be a terrible damn problem. Frankly, these people frighten me. Politics and governing demand compromise. But these Christians believe they are acting in the name of God, so they can't and won't compromise. I know, I've tried to deal with them." -- Barry Goldwater

-----

"Where free unions and collective bargaining are forbidden, freedom is lost." -- President Ronald Reagan (1911-2004), Labor Day speech at Jersey City, New Jersey, September 1, 1980

"We establish no religion in this country. We command no worship. We mandate no belief, nor will we ever. Church and state are and must remain separate." -- Ronald Reagan

-----

WAR, MILITARISM

"I have seen war. I have seen war on land and sea. I have seen blood running from the wounded. I have seen men coughing out their gassed lungs. I have seen the dead in the mud. I have seen cities destroyed.... I have seen children starving. I have seen the agony of mothers and wives. I hate war." -- President Franklin Delano Roosevelt (1882-1945), speech at Chautauqua, New York, Aug. 14, 1936

"I am tired and sick of war. Its glory is all moonshine. It is only those who have neither fired a shot nor heard the shrieks and groans of the wounded who cry aloud for blood, more vengeance, more desolation. War is hell." -- General William Tecumseh Sherman (1820-1891)

"Every gun that is made, every warship launched, every rocket fired, signifies, in the final sense, a theft from those who hunger and are not fed, those who are cold and are not clothed. This world in arms is not spending money alone. It is spending the sweat of its laborers, the genius of its scientists, the hopes of its children. The cost of one modern heavy bomber is this: a modern brick school in more than 30 cities. It is two electric power plants, each serving a town of 60,000 population. It is two fine, fully-equipped hospitals. It is some 50 miles of concrete highway. We pay for a single fighter plane with a half-million bushels of wheat. We pay for a single destroyer with new homes that could have housed more than 8,000 people." -- President Dwight Eisenhower (1890-1969), address to American Society of Newspaper Editors, April 16, 1953.

"War is just a racket.... It is conducted for the benefit of the very few at the expense of the masses. I spent 33 years and four months in active military service, and during that period I spent most of my time as a high-class thug for Big Business, for Wall Street and the bankers. In short, I was a racketeer, a gangster for capitalism. Like all the members of the military profession, I never had a thought of my own until I left the service. My mental faculties remained in suspended animation while I obeyed the orders of higher-ups. This is typical with everyone in the military service." -- Retired Marine General Smedley Butler (1881-1940), two-time winner of the Congressional Medal of Honor, in a 1933 speech.

"You can't say civilization doesn't advance.... In every war they kill you a new way." -- Mark Twain (1835-1910)

"I know war as few other men now living know it, and nothing to me is more revolting. I have long advocated its complete abolition, as its very destructiveness to both friend and foe has rendered it useless as a method of settling international disputes." -- General Douglas

MacArthur (1880-1964), farewell speech to Congress, April 19, 1951

"You can no more win a war than you can win an earthquake." -- Rep. Jeanette Rankin (1880-1973), from her biography, *First Lady in Congress*, 1974

"Older men declare war. But it is the youth that must fight and die. And it is youth who must inherit the tribulation, the sorrow, and the triumphs that follow the aftermath of war." -- President Herbert Hoover (1874-1964)

"War never slays a bad man in its course, but the good always.... War loves to prey upon the young." -- Sophocles (c. 496-406 BCE)

"There never was a good war or a bad peace." -- Benjamin Franklin (1706-1790)

"Since war begins in the minds of men, it is in the minds of men that we must begin to erect the ramparts of peace." -- UNESCO charter

-----

"Ez for war, I call it murder / There you have it, plain and flat / I don't want to go no furder / Than my testyment for that." -- James Russell Lowell (1819-1891)

"My enemy is dead, a man divine as myself." -- Walt Whitman (1819-1892)

"Wars are not 'acts of God.' They are caused by man, by man-made institutions, by the way in which man has organized his society. What man has made, man can change." -- Supreme Court Chief Justice Fred M. Vinson (1890-1953)

"We cannot dedicate -- we cannot consecrate -- we cannot hallow this ground. The brave men, living and dead, who struggled here, have consecrated it far above our poor power to add or detract. The world will little note, nor long remember, what we say here, but it can never forget what they did here. It is for us the living, rather, to be dedicated here to the unfinished work which they who fought here have thus far so nobly advanced. It is rather for us to be dedicated to the great task remaining before us -- that from these honored dead we take increased devotion to that cause for which they gave the last full measure of devotion -- that we here highly resolve that these dead shall not have died in vain; that this nation, under God, shall have a new birth of freedom; and the government of the people, by the people, for the people, shall not perish from the earth." -- Abraham Lincoln (1809-1865), dedicating the Civil War battlefield cemetery at Gettysburg, 1863

"There are few die well that die in a battle." -- William Shakespeare (1564-1616), *Henry V*

"Doughboys were paid a whole dollar a day / and received free burial under the clay / And movie heroes are paid even more / shooting one another in a Hollywood war." -- American poet and Liberal Club member Alfred Kreymborg (1883-1966), *What Price Glory?*

"I find a hundred thousand sorrows touching my heart, and there is ringing in my ears like an admonition eternal, an insistent call, 'It must not be again.'" -- President Warren Harding (1865-1923) at Hoboken, over bodies of American Expeditionary Force soldiers returned from France in World War I

"It takes 20 years or more of peace to make a man; it takes only 20 seconds of war to destroy him." -- King Baudoin I (1930-1993) of Belgium, addressing America's Congress in 1959

"Terrible as an army with banners." -- *The Song of Solomon*

"In peace, children inter their parents; war violates the order of nature, and causes parents to inter their children." -- Herodotus (c. 485-425 BCE)

"One murder makes a villain, millions a hero." -- English bishop and slavery abolitionist Beilby Porteus (1731-1809)

"The sword sung on the barren heath, the sickle in the fruitful field; the sword he sung a song of death, but could not make the sickle yield." -- mystical English poet William Blake (1757-1827)

"'You're wounded!' 'Nay,' the soldier's pride / touched to the quick, he said / 'I'm killed, Sire!' and his chief beside / smiling the boy fell dead." -- English poet Robert Browning (1812-1889)

"Wars throughout history have been waged for conquest and plunder.... The working class who fight all the battles, the working class who make the supreme sacrifices, the working class who freely shed their blood and furnish the corpses, have never yet had a voice in either declaring war or making peace. It is the ruling class that invariably does both. They alone declare war and they alone make peace.... They are continually talking about your patriotic duty. It is not their, but your, patriotic duty that they are concerned about. There is a decided difference. Their patriotic duty never takes them to the firing line or chucks them into the trenches." -- socialist-pacifist-labor leader Eugene V. Debs (1855-1926), part of a 1918 speech at Canton, Ohio, that caused him to be sentenced to ten years in prison under the Sedition Act

-----

"War hath no fury like a non-combatant."
-- British journalist Charles Edward Montague
(1867-1928), *Disenchantment,* 1922

"The appalling thing about war is that it kills all love of truth." -- Danish critic Georg Brandes (1842-1927), letter to French Prime Minister Georges Clemenceau, 1915

"Is there any man here, or any woman -- let me say, is there any child -- who does not know that the seed of war in the modern world is industrial and commercial rivalry?" - President Woodrow Wilson (1856-1924), speech in St. Louis, September 5, 1919

"The painful paradox is that fighting for one's country can render one unfit to be its citizen.... War changes you... strips you of all your beliefs, your religion, takes your dignity away, you become an animal." -- Jonathan Shay, *Achilles in Vietnam: Combat Traumas and the Undoing of Character*

"Military justice is to justice as military music is to music." -- witty French Prime Minister Georges Clemenceau (1841-1929)

James A. Haught is longtime editor of West Virginia's largest newspaper, *The Charleston Gazette-Mail*, where he has won two dozen national newswriting awards. He has written eleven books and 100 magazine essays. He is in *Who's Who in America*, *Who's Who in the World, Contemporary Authors*, and *2000 Outstanding Intellectuals of the 21st Century*.

In 2015, he wrote three columns about the historic record of liberal political victories that transformed Western civilization and established today's society. The columns were distributed by two syndicates and appeared in a total of 130 U.S. newspapers. They became the foundation of this book.

Web site: http://haught.net.

E-mail: haught@wvgazettemail.com

Phone: (304) 348-5199

Fax: (304) 348-1233

Postal: Charleston Gazette-Mail, 1001 Virginia St. E., Charleston, WV 25301

Previous books by Haught:

Holy Horrors: An Illustrated History of Religious Murder and Madness - (Prometheus Books, 1990). Translated into Spanish as *Horror Sagrado*, Turkish as *Kutsal Dehpet*, Portuguese as *Persguicoes Religiosas*, and Polish as *Swiety Koszmar*.

Science in a Nanosecond: Illustrated Answers to 100 Basic Science Questions - (Prometheus, 1990). Translated into Polish as *Nauka w Nanosekunde* and Italian as *Il Vuoto di Torricelli.*

The Art of Lovemaking: An Illustrated Tribute - (Prometheus, 1992). A gallery of lovers by major artists, showing the beauty of sex, countering both church taboos and the crudity of pornographers.

Holy Hatred: Religious Conflicts of the '90s - (Prometheus, 1995). Translated into Japanese by Jiji Press, 1996, into Turkish as *Kutsal Nephret* and into Spanish as *Odio Sagrado.*

2,000 Years of Disbelief: Famous People With the Courage to Doubt - (Prometheus, 1996).

Holy Horrors (expanded paperback after 9/11) - (Prometheus, 2002).

Honest Doubt: Essays on Atheism in a Believing Society - (Prometheus, 2007).

Amazon Moon, a freethought novel of fabled women warriors, citing religious sacrifices, oracles and Sacred Wars in ancient Greece - (BookLocker, 2007).

Fascinating West Virginia: Wild, Memorable Episodes From the Longtime Editor of the Mountain State's Largest Newspaper - (Charleston Gazette, 2008)

Fading Faith: The Rise of the Secular Age - (Gustav Broukal Press, 2010)

Religion is Dying: Soaring Secularism in America and the West - (CreateSpace, 2014)